The Elderly
Uncooperative Patient

The Elderly Uncooperative Patient

Edited by
T.L. Brink

The Haworth Press
New York • London

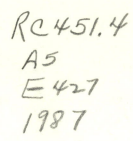

The Elderly Uncooperative Patient has also been published as *Clinical Gerontologist*, Volume 6, Number 2, Winter 1986.

The Haworth Press, Inc. 12 West 32 Street, New York, NY 10001
EUROSPAN/Haworth, 3 Henrietta Street, London WC2E 8LU England

Library of Congress Cataloging-in-Publication Data

The Elderly uncooperative patient.

    Includes bibliographies and index.
    "Has also been published as Clinical gerontologist, volume 6, number 2, winter 1986"—T.p. verso.
    1. Geriatric psychiatry. 2. Patient compliance. 3. Cooperativeness.
4. Psychotherapist and patient. I. Brink, T. L. (Terry L.) [DNLM:
1. Aged—psychology. 2. Hospitalization—in old age. 3. Patient Compliance.
4. Physician-Patient Relations. 5. Psychotherapy—in old age.
W1 CL71D v.6 no. 2/ WT 150 E37]
RC451.4.A5E427 1986   618.97'0019   86-26997
ISBN 0-86656-604-X

The Elderly Uncooperative Patient

Clinical Gerontologist
Volume 6, Number 2

CONTENTS

Clinical Gerontologist

Preface

This project began as a special issue of the journal, *Clinical Gerontologist*. Therefore, there are frequent editor's references to previous articles published in *CG* on similar topics. Indeed, previous issues have contained articles and clinical comments which alluded to uncooperative patients under the rubrics of

aggressive behavior
  III (1) 51–52
  III (3) 36–39
  III (4) 78–80

hostility
  III (1) 22–23
  III (2) 5–10

problem behaviors
  II (2) 23–37
  II (4) 70–72
  III (1) 61–62, 64–68
  III (2) 41–43

For this issue only, our review sections have been deleted and we have integrated articles and shorter clinical comments in order to preserve continuity of topical development.

Regular readers of the journal are assured that the next issue of *CG* will be a regular issue, containing our usual potpourri of articles and clinical comments on a broad range of subjects, in addition to reviews of relevant books and other media.

TLB

xi

The Elderly Uncooperative Patient

SECTION ONE:
UNDERSTANDING AND ASSESSING UNCOOPERATIVENESS

Chapter 1:
Who's to Blame for Uncooperativeness?

Burr places the blame squarely on the shoulder of mental health clinicians: psychiatrists, psychologists, social workers, and nurses, who "write off" geriatric cases as hopeless. Actually, we have too many cases of self-fulfilling prophecy: the clinician's assumption of untreatability becomes translated into a patient who resists treatment.

Burr attempts to get us into the mind frame of the patient. Uncooperative behavior can be viewed as active resistance, a defensive action which serves to preserve self-esteem and ward off the invasiveness of intervention conducted by an unsympathetic therapist. Resistance is therefore a sign of strength, and a vain attempt to defiantly compensate for real declines in autonomy and functional capacity.

The therapeutic solution is not to confront resistance, but to honor it. Indeed, this may be the only way to establish the therapeutic relationship. Once established, the key is to pay attention to the uniqueness of the patient's needs and life style: being directive, or non-directive, as appropriate, and being ever so cautious not to rekindle the fear or anger which will reinstitute uncooperativeness.

Burr presents a case study of an 82 year old woman, and demonstrates the need for adopting the patient's irrational rationale rather than trying to prematurely argue it away. Another case of a 79 year old man demonstrates the need for the therapist to be perceived as an ally in the patient's angry denunciations of the staff.

The Patient As Hero: A Psychotherapeutic Approach to Work With Resistant Aged Patients

Helen Turner Burr, PhD, ACSW

Clinicians who work with declining elderly patients or clients generally mute their expectations for therapeutic success and foresee a slow pace towards even limited goals. Such patients and clients usually offer no dramatic rewards. When additionally these patients fail to cooperate with our efforts to help them, we may have the set-up for a psychological wrestling match as, to mix metaphors, they drag their feet down the therapeutic path. Their psychological motivations for failing to cooperate need to be seriously considered when we undertake to serve or treat these troubling patients. Voluntary aged patients, almost as often as the involuntary, seem to evade or sabotage our treatment efforts. Why this should be has become of increasing interest to clinicians, practitioners, therapists. (The terms for these professionals will be used interchangeably, as with patient and client.)

THEORETICAL FRAMEWORK FOR A PSYCHOTHERAPEUTIC APPROACH

The prevalent view of uncooperative patient behavior, understandably stemming from the clinician's impatient reactions, is that of willful and foolish obstruction to direction from others, or to acknowledgment of the need for change on his part; disbelief in the therapist; passive or open uncooperativeness; or purely negativistic meanness of character. A less common but more strongly emerging view regards the aged

5

patient's resistant behavior from the patient's standpoint, more as a sign of perhaps misdirected but promising strength; defensive action against giving in to threatening impairments and against demands on him for attempting something new and strange which he may feel he cannot do.

Viewing uncooperative behavior as active resistance can paradoxically reduce the scope of the struggle with the patient from battle to strategy which calls for wit rather than force. Psychotherapeutic success then can be achieved not by defeating the patient but outwitting him, by winning him over to the treatment or service goal by making it his own choice. This concept of resistance will be elaborated later.

Effective approaches with a clinician's clients, acquiescent or not, mentally intact or not, depend on the quality of the interchange between them. A few conclusions from experience are noted.

1. Relationship therapy appears most effective with the frail aged. This therapeutic relationship, often possible to establish with most patients in a first meeting together, needs to be established differently with hostile or resistant patients.
2. In their interchanges, psychodynamics reign-comment and interpretation, suggestion and response, exploration and discovery, action and reaction.
3. A good outcome with aged patients requires great sensitivity to their desires as well as to their fears for themselves, and dedication to their right to self-direction in spite of increasing helplessness and dependency.

Whatever form his resistance takes it is particularly important to sustain the failing aged patient's sense of personal identity, his intactness as an individual, as his capacities and accustomed resources fade; to assert with him and for him his right to direct his own life; and to bolster his sense of mastery over his own life direction, even in the face of his actual impotence. This psychotherapeutic relationship task, of course, influences how one deals with his avoidance of or refusal to acknowledge decline, and with his resistance to accepting proffered help.

Psychotherapeutic efforts with functionally-impaired aged

patients and clients, whether they be resistant or cooperative, are uniquely complicated by the patient's emotional devastation over his sense of helplessness and dependency, however expressed, in the train of his real decline in functioning. Additionally, work with such individuals is commonly bedeviled by the presence or suspicion of brain damage which can impair their contribution to the treatment relationship and to the treatment process. Both emotional and mental problems play their part in the resistant behavior patterns we see and to which we react.

Resistance in aged patients and clients may be considered, however, as a sign of strength and defiance of outer assaults on their integrity as individuals, and it can be utilized psychodynamically to further the therapeutic process. The themes enunciated above, of dignifying the role of resistance in aged patients, understanding the emotional basis for it, and reacting psychodynamically in the interpersonal treatment exchanges, will be further discussed.

RESISTANCE AS A CONCEPT

Resistance is a more pliant concept of the patient's behavior than uncooperativeness, which may emphasize the patient's weakness, passive lag or failure to move, and so overlook the strong, active, defensive-aggressive aspect. Neither lack of cooperation nor resistance are particularly pleasant behaviors to deal with, but "resistance" is the author's view encompasses a livelier, more attractive concept than uncooperativeness and one which can psychodynamically shape a more mutually engaging and rewarding treatment process. We should take heart from the hints in current medical research that a fighting spirit may be healthier than quiet stoicism.

Additionally—perhaps fundamentally—the view of any kind of resistance as active behavior allows opportunity psychologically to show appropriate respect for the resistant client's values and wishes as a focus in the service relationship. The care taken in weighing these client values and behavior can also serve diagnostically to delineate the boundaries beyond which authoritative protection rather than psychotherapeutic measures alone must be invoked. Yet, especially when the client is brain-damaged and beyond rational reach, a therapeutic relationship may be all he can respond to emotionally and the only service that can sustain him in the face of destruction of his integrity.

Honoring his resistance to further invasion of his personal integrity and joining in his desire to remain his own man may be the only way to establish a helping bond, even if perceived by the angry patient as beating the therapist in a contest of wills. Where the resistance is so great as to permit only one or two sessions, and the patient remains adamant against any proffered service or continued contract, he can still be helped—bolstered up psychologically—by open acknowledgement of his resoluteness, even though the therapist must sigh over the patient's self-defeating behavior.

RIDING THE PSYCHODYNAMIC SEE-SAW

As in any treatment relationship, the clinician directs or aims the psychodynamic transactions between himself and the patient to elicit significant material and to demonstrate his healing, protective intent. Psychodynamics, the process of balancing action and reaction in the therapeutic interchange, is used more as a strategy which creates directed movement than as a prescriptive theory.

In this interactive climate and manner of communicating, the therapist guides the direction of their discussion out of what the patient brings up, and also regulates the balance between the emotional and rational. The effect is to bring the patient's erratic highs and lows, or swinging to extremes, to a more stable rest, conclusion, balance.

The psychotherapeutic maneuvers involved are like a see-saw in the reactions and responses to the matters the patient and practitioner toss back and forth between them. Violent ups and downs will not be a pleasant experience. If in the balancing act the therapist is too precipitous, too controlling, he can by his greater weight keep the resistant patient dangling helplessly in the air or bring him to the ground in a frightening crash. The patient must have some power, some weight, to help come to a possible balance. In psychodynamic interaction where both are actors, there is reciprocity, mutual reliance on a sense of safety because each can consensually touch ground and control bounce, and even feel adventure in the process.

The see-saw concept, perhaps overdrawn, is nevertheless useful to demonstrate the importance of the personal dignity and rights of the patient which must not be outweighed or discredited by his therapist or his society, if a truly equable, satisfying and stimulating psychotherapeutic outcome is to be achieved.

In short, the psychodynamic approach is one of give and take on both sides, a strategic modification of the clinician's insistent drive to control and of the impaired and needy old client's unrealistic stand against accommodating to losses in functioning and to necessary changes. Otherwise, on one hand giving in to his resistance, permitting him to persist against the encroaching future without attempting a bond, means a failure of psychotherapeutic effort. At the other extreme, where the helpless client is forced to submit to the clinician's imperatives, the therapist's arrogant authoritarianism obliterates the client's remaining measure of mastery. (This dynamic is not to be confused with submissive, manipulative client behavior in search of open protection.) Such approaches differ from sensing and, importantly, responding to the resistant client's fearful perception of the treatment scene, the obliteration of his will, which has led to his unwillingness to engage in mutual planning or to accept support.

OF MANNER AND METHOD

How can practitioners avoid or reduce excessive resistance and attain mutual investment in the service plan? The patient's innate character and level of dependency, as well as the facade he wishes to show, will help determine whether the ultimate psychotherapeutic goal is to support, sustain, or protect him. These factors and the patient's personality can help the clinician to employ the appropriate interactive feints— whether and when to "cajole, preach, thunder, joke, stonewall, surrender"—and to decide how to draw the patient into the action and movement.

Face to face with the client, the practitioner has many

methods he can use selectively or in turn, depending on the patient and the stage in the therapeutic process. He can confer, advise, persuade, inform, order, For example:

—He can review the patient's situation and alternative advantageous changes, and advise on what he thinks is best for the patient;

—He can select the alternative and make the choice for the patient, and persuade him to go along;

—He can argue against the patient's choices which he opposes;

—He can explain what he would like the patient to accept by relying on persuasive reassurances of his own continuing protection;

—He can use his personal charm and the patient's trust seductively to elicit unconditional acceptance or agreement to his suggestions.

These strategies obviously cover a range of patient role and cooperativeness. Their uses may be justified in effecting necessary changes least painfully for the patient while conserving his psychological, if not physical, survival.

The cooperative patient will assume that the clinician's advice is probably right, and in his own interest will attempt to adopt his advisor's point of view or follow his direction; with the uncooperative patient the therapist may also be right but, alas, the patient disagrees that his advisor's proposals are in his interest. The range of psychotherapeutic strategies available to use with trusting, accepting patients is then curtailed by the uncooperative patient's resistance to giving up his own sense of control and to give ground. Who wins? Who gives in? Is there such a thing as victory? Whose fight is it anyhow? In any case, it is honest and helpful to acknowledge the gallantry of the embattled patient who goes down fighting.

ENCOUNTERING RESISTANCE

Two cases are presented to illustrate common types of resistance in older impaired patients and specific therapeutic responses to them. The first case deals with a frightened woman in a brief psychotic episode, the second, with an explosively angry and impotent man. Both fear and anger appear to underlie the behavior of each. In both cases communication follows a psychodynamic pattern; but what is conveyed to each is markedly different. The patients' distortions of reality serve not only as a coping technique but also as hostile expression.

In the first case, we see fear as resistance.

THE FRIGHTENED CRAZY WOMAN

I may cite a deceptively slight instance of psychodynamic interaction with a fierce old lady caught in the terror of her own decline. This 82-year-old widow is a European-born artist, intact intellectually but the only survivor of a family wiped out in the Nazi regime. Twice thereafter she was displaced and dislocated from her roots; successful in adapting to foreign lands and languages, in supporting her ineffectual husband, in bringing up her daughter, and in achieving some local renown for her paintings. Eight years ago her daughter, who had settled in the United States, forcibly brought her here from Mexico because of her mother's psychotic episode brought on by a friend's attempted suicide in her presence. I have seen the patient regularly for several years during which she has been hospitalized twice for short episodes of psychotic depression. With this highly bred patient, conventional patterns of polite social interchange and formal interpersonal transactions impeded easy examination of her emotionally bloody wounds, the extraordinary demand of the psychotherapeutic relationship. She is chronically agitated and depressed, but responsive to our close warm relationship which she craves.

At this time she is again in the hospital for psychotic agitation/depression, after a minor auto accident in which she had been hurt. I am called in this afternoon because since her admission she has adamantly refused to eat or talk with the resident psychiatrist. When I see her she is frozen in manner but responsive to my sharing her catastrophic reactions. She is then able to reestablish her intimate connection with me and and to confide her secret conviction—she has not told this to hospital staff or her daughter—that she is imprisoned in a Nazi concentration camp, that the food they give her is poisoned, that her daughter has been bamboozled by the doctor who is actually Dr. Mengele in disguise.

The proper therapeutic-psychodynamic response is, obviously, not to argue her idea down or to scold her for her "uncooperativeness" and refusal of care. Instead, I say: If what she says is true, what other ways could she get food? Would she eat her daughter's cooking if the daughter would bring it in? This possibility engages her and calms her agitation somewhat. She thinks of other possibilities, which we talk over, and how realistically these plans could be managed. Suddenly she mentions her feelings of catastrophe when she had had the recent automobile accident.

I say, this violence you experienced reminded you of the violence done to your family in the war, of your family's murders. It must have made you feel the way they must have felt. She agrees; this is true. That is why she is so upset, over these recollections. I ask if these reawakened fears of the Nazis through her own dangerous accident might make her imagine they have captured her now, and are poisoning her food to kill her? (Maybe . . .) but perhaps her imagination is not real? It is her own terrible feelings that made her forget where she really is now? As an artist she uses her imagination so much. . . . She responds slowly, pleased by my compliment; possibly so, maybe so; but she does not think this is her imagination. My response: we will see. I leave her to cogitate this possibility and to decide if she will ask her daughter to bring in her meals.

A short follow-up visit the next day finds her still anxious but less agitated, and she confesses she had accepted breakfast this morning. She agrees she should test how she feels by lunch time; if she feels okay, perhaps she can rely on the hospital?—concentration camp— food, especially if her daughter will join her at lunch and eat with her. Shortly thereafter she has recovered and can be discharged.

Although vulnerable to bouts of profound depression especially at anniversaries, holidays, and news accounts of honoring Holocaust victims, our weekly sessions seem to be maintaining her and she is now attempting water-colors to please me and surprise her daughter.

In this case, adopting the patient's irrational rationale instead of arguing it down makes it possible to deal with it in a reasoning manner and the resistance gives way.

This matter-of-fact recounting of a minor incident is neither a spectacular nor unusual event in the experience of most therapists. However, the telling does not reflect sufficiently the enormous need of the resistant aged patient or client for exchanging confidences or repressed feelings he or she is ter-rified to face alone, or even to express. Seemingly irrational resistant behavior has got to be the overlay for soul-shaking emotion, linked perhaps irrationally but with some internal logic to the past.

A look at another manifestation of resistance to cover up helplessness suggests a very different approach for bestowing a sense of power which can diminish the combatant patient's need to fight for it. A "social conflict" (Cingolani, 1984) struggle of direct confrontation with such patients, although contrary to much traditional social work teaching, may some-times be effective in helping involuntary or hostile patients who seem intractible, if used initially to establish the power and authority of the therapist to harm or help. Then allowing the patient to overcome this powerful figure in interviews can reestablish the patient's own feelings of strength and he can then use the therapist's power for his own ends. A dependent but characteristically defiant patient can even enjoy as well as benefit from the pleasures of a struggle which he feels he has won. The case of a severely impaired impotent angry man illustrates this process (Turner, 1960).

THE ANGRY CRIPPLE

A 79-year-old retired seaman, who had roamed the world as a misfit, a life-long misanthrope and alcoholic, suffered a stroke after three years of chronically angry residence in a home for the aged. He blamed the stroke on medical neglect and inept therapy of an originally minor complaint. His apopletic behavior in the nursing unit over the next two years had grown more and more intransigent, resistive and abusive. He refused stubbornly to take medications, then to participate in rehabilitation treatment, and finally to walk or move by himself. He constantly accused the staff of abusing him. When he began to strike out with his cane at nurses and orderlies attempting to attend to him, he was referred to the psychiatrist.

In the first two very brief sessions the psychiatrist interrogated him about his angry and uncontrolled behavior in a manner he saw as disapproving, prohibitive, threatening, powerful, authoritarian. In the third session he angrily denounced the doctors, the home, the nurses, and especially the psychiatrist. In response, the psychiatrist appeared suitably distressed, cautiously self-defensive, and semi-apologetic without ever admitting that the patient was right in his complaints. After ten minutes of denunciation and this receptive response, it was tactfully agreed that he could take his leave.

He departed with an air of righteous indignation, triumphant. For the next few days he was relatively silent and cheerful on his ward, and there were no angry outbursts; his attitude was that of one who has bearded the lion in his den and emerged victorious. He was contemptuous of the harmful potentialities of those about him and submitted to their ministrations without protest. A further opportunity for him to vent his anger at staff and psychiatrist and to emerge triumphant, was offered in the next five-minute interview about a week later.

In this fourth interview—two weeks after the first—the patient came to the session for the first time in street clothes, which he had helped don himself. His attitude was also changed: he now seemed to feel safe with the "defeated" therapist, who appeared none the worse for wear. He spoke angrily of the staff and his plight, but as to an ally. The therapist listened sympathetically, suggested that the patient could probably do a great deal to rectify matters despite the opposition which he felt existed, and offered to prescribe a new medication for one of his complaints.

Following this, there was, according to the needs of the patient, a shifting of the therapist's role-playing between that of the strong parent who can be vanquished and that of the strong parental ally. After four months and eight interviews that was noticeable improvement in his behavior and a shift from angry immobility on his part to relatively peaceful although limited ambulation.

In summary: This man, whose lifelong feelings of helplessness were reinforced by hemiplegia and the concomitant effects of brain injury, had handled the anxiety thus generated by an angry show of force. This was ineffective in overcoming his fear and, in fact, increased his retaliation fear. In this setting he was depressed, immobile, and explosively angry. The therapist stepped in to provide him with an illusion of omnipotence through triumph over a powerful, threatening physician. Some of the omnipotent feelings could only be short-lived, but they were later replaced by acceptance of the "defeated" therapist as a powerful parental ally. Safely entrenched with him, the patient's helplessness decreased, his anxiety diminished, and reparative rage was unnecessary; so that there was simultaneous improvement in behavior and decrease of his suffering. His dependence on this relationship was demonstrated when in the therapist's temporary absence the staff was unable to substitute for the special therapeutic relationship, the patient returned to violent behavior, and was transferred to a mental hospital.

Some form of relationship therapy is required in dispensing any kind of service if the help offered—material or psychosocial—is not to violate the recipient's pride. The practitioner must offer more than opportunity for rapport; he must extend himself to give parental love and permissiveness in the guise most acceptable to his aged patient. The practitioner may perceive the demands this deal makes on him more keenly than the demands for sharing he makes on the suffering patient.

But, recall, to the defensive failure, means "the recapitulation not only of all his sins but also of all his fugitive and fallen dreams (Kennedy, 1983). We require from the old resistant one that he open this dangerous Pandora's box, expose his most deeply-buried secrets to us, hurtful personal revelations; we expect him after all his years to divulge the distorted shape of his life, his own shameful nature, the bitter distillations of his living. We should be aware of what our tearing open his guarded secrets costs him, and the value of his insights, which we can hold as inheritance from his life's experience.

If one can go beyond considering resistance as a sign of weakness and cowardice to face reality we may find these old patients, still in armor, more heroic than they or we usually have opportunity to recognize. Even if we have no satisfactory answers for most of the clients we see in the last years of their lives, we can offer a reflective gentleness, protective warmth in the form they recognize, humor to restore their perspectives, reduction in anxiety and sense of isolation, admiration, and an agreeable interaction which invites affection as well as a sharing of the ironies and wonders of life. Then we both win; if not the battle with dying, then at least the final skirmish before the end.

REFERENCES

Cingolani, J. Social Conflict Perspective on Work With Involuntary Clients. *Social Work,* 1984, *29,* 442–446.
Kennedy, W. *Ironweed.* New York: Penguin Books, 1983.
Turner, H. The Patient as a Person in the Treatment Relationship. *Journal of Health and Human Services,* 1960, *1,* 278–284.

Chapter 2:
The Role of Depression and Anger

Peterson contends that anger and depression are possible factors underlying uncooperativeness. Anger can result in active or passive resistance to therapeutic progress while depression merely reduces the patient's capacity of cope. Peterson concludes that there is more hope with anger than depression, for with the former, at least the strength of the patient is mobilized, albeit in a negative fashion. It is easier to turn the negative mobilization into a positive one than to start from the nothingness of depression.

A case is presented: an 88 year old man denied he was depressed, yet exhibited many of the classic symptoms. It was only when his depression was replaced with anger (at the staff) that he became communicative and animated. Peterson demonstrated a good deal of skill as a therapist in converting that anger into a more positive, social feeling.

Previous *CG* issues have discussed issues related to anger, such as agitation:

I (3) 45–52
I (4) 74–75
III (1) 50–52

Rx: Anger

Lizette Peterson, PhD

Anger and depression are two of the most common etiologies for uncooperativeness in a geriatric patient. Anger can result in either passive aggression toward therapy or active attempts to thwart progress. Depression, on the other hand, may simply sap the elderly patient's motivation for change, making progress slow and sluggish, or even absent. These factors thus seem to exert opposite types of influence on a patient, with anger pushing against progress and depression pulling against positive movement. In the present case study, I want to discuss an unusual interaction between these two factors. Specifically, I will describe the use of anger as a vehicle for reducing depression-related uncooperativeness in a geriatric medical patient. I believe the technique is valuable to outline, but that it should be employed judiciously and only when more conventional methods have failed.

The patient, Mr. G., was an 88 year old gentleman with congestive heart failure. He had been hospitalized for over two weeks at the time of the referral and his physical disease was under medical control. He had been referred to me by his physician, who felt that Mr. G.'s complaints of lack of energy and his general disinterest in physical therapy, meals, and visits from relatives were due to emotional rather than physical dysfunction. Mr. G. had also been uncooperative with the nursing staff. He was eating poorly and preferred to remain flat on his back, despite the reiterated concern that pneumonia could develop if he did not spend some portion of his time sitting upright. He refused to ambulate at all, demanding a bedside urinal instead, even though he was capable to walking and it was a necessary part of his recovery.

Although Mr. G. explicitly denied being depressed, state-

Dr. Peterson is with the University of Missouri-Columbia.

ments like "I came to the hospital to die, only the doctors won't let me" and "I'm nothing but a burden to my children" were consistent with a diagnosis of depression, as were his sleeping and eating disturbances and general affect. Mr. G. was not only uncooperative with eating, ambulation, and physical therapy but he was unwilling to be involved in any attempts to alter his mood or to reinvolve himself with the world. I had tried a gamut of techniques from sensitive-empathetic to briskly business-like, but Mr. G. would plead that he was too tired to talk that day, that it was of no use, or that my time would be better spent with the younger patients on the ward who could still look forward to a full life. Mr. G.'s poor eyesight made reading and television unrewarding, he reported, but he also resisted the use of tape-recorded stories and music obtained for him. Even sitting quietly together failed to build rapport. Mr. G. could stare fixedly out of the window for hours on end, refusing to communicate.

One morning a new aide on the ward awakened Mr. G. Without his false teeth in place and still dazed from sleep, Mr. G. seemed incoherent to the aide who, ignoring Mr. G.'s muted protests, lifted him out of bed and into a wheelchair, meanwhile murmuring what the aide assumed to be consoling reminders of the the name of the hospital, the city in which it was located, the current date, and the fact that the linen in the room needed changing and the floor needed to be mopped. In the meantime, Mr. G. would enjoy a nice sit in the hall.

Mr. G. was accustomed to the nursing staff's pleading and cajoling, and my—at least externally—patient and responsive stance. Being unceremoniously dumped into a wheelchair ("I'm not paralyzed, you know. I've still got the use of my legs!"), wheeled out into the public hallway in his hospital gown ("Couldn't have been more than 60 degrees out there and I'm sitting there with my personal parts in the breeze!"), left there for a prolonged period of time ("I must have been there for three hours, with everyone ignoring me"), and most of all, being spoken to as if he were senile ("Talked to me like I was a baby! Did I know where I was? I sure as hell knew more than that kid did!") enraged him. And, surprisingly, an enraged Mr. G. was apparently a more adaptive individual.

When I came by with my daily "want to talk about anything?" I was greeted by a new man. Color in his cheeks, fire in his eyes, sitting erect without nursing staff entreaties, he told me about the dreadful way he had been treated. This outrage lasted for two days, during which time Mr. G. was active and verbal. Then Mr. G. began sliding back toward apathy and hopelessness. On the third day, I again found him lying flat on his back (against medical advice) and "too tired" to talk to me. Taking a deep mental breath, I replied that if he were too exhausted or confused to talk, I could return later when his mind seemed more clear. Instantly, I had a willing conversational partner, ready to testily explain to me that confusion had nothing to do with it. I elevated his bed and we did some good work in the next hour.

In spite of this initially positive impact, I felt the anger could be as problematic as the depression in the long run. Although for the next week it served an eliciting function, I worked furiously to replace it with a more adaptive vehicle. Individuals like the aide made mistakes because of a lack of knowledge of the elderly and their abilities, I pointed out. There was a lot of educating to be done with most people. Perhaps a handout could be written. . . but by whom? Mr. G.'s failing eyesight did allow him to write in a large wavering script. Following the completion of the project, he wrote a piece on the secrets to a successful 40 year marriage and after that, he wrote about some important family memories for his children. Nursing staff reminders and the provision of a desk with paper down the hall increased ambulation. The anger, although sometimes still present, was largely replaced by a new reaction toward feeling useless; Mr. G.'s more typical desire to help others.

Again, because anger is a potentially destructive and dangerous emotion, it should be used as a therapeutic vehicle sparingly and judiciously, never before trying more conventional techniques. However, as a method of breaking through depression to reach the elderly patient, this technique would seem to have promise.

Chapter 3
Make the Patient Feel Like a Helper

Gropper reports on the case of a 58 year old woman who proved unco-operative during outpatient assessment procedures. He astutely inferred that her uncooperativeness was attributable to diminished self-esteem and sense of helplessness. Perplexed by how to get the patient to return for the completion of assessment, Gropper came up with a brilliant idea; tell the patient that data from "brighter" patients are needed for a research project. This approach not only secured compliance, but it conveyed to the patient that the examiner had respect for her intelligence, and gave her the chance to help someone else.

The issue of how to secure patient compliance in the testing process was the topic of a previous clinical comment in *CG:*

III (3) 40–41

Strategic Oneupmanship:
A Technique for Managing
the Uncooperative Client

Robert Gropper, PhD

From 1979 through 1984, at the Epilepsy Foundation of South Florida over two hundred clients were seen for neuro-educational testing. The typical adult battery included a brief patient history which was gathered both from the file and through an interview with the subject. The tests administered included the WAIS, Bender-Gestalt, Rotter Locus of Control, Peabody Picture Vocabulary Test, and the Washington Psychosocial Inventory.

The entire procedure would be done during two appointments and typically take between two and three hours. An educational psychologist and social worker worked together in this process. The results of these tests would be used in a number of ways; to determine patient eligibility for federally funded services, to develop rehabilitation plans and to aid the staff in providing therapy.

The combination of organic involvement, drug interaction, and anxiety of dealing with professionals who could determine future financial benefits sometimes made for awkward moments (e.g., Gran Mal and psychomotor seizures accompanied by agressive and antisocial behavior). A particularly difficult case was referred to the foundation for an evaluation and recommendations.

Mildred R., a white female, was first seen in 1981. At that time she was fifty-eight years old and living with an older sister. There was no reported family history of epilepsy. Her mother had been briefly institutionalized for a psychiatric disorder. Mildred had a twelfth grade education. She was unem-

Dr. Gropper is with the University of Miami.

ployed for the last eight years. Before that she worked as a dressmaker and pattern designer, but had to retire because of her physical and psychological problems. The onset of her convulsive disorder began about the age of twenty-six after a car accident in which she received right temporal lobe damage. She had been seizure-free for almost two years prior to this evaluation. Her medication included Dilantin, Tegratol, and occasional small doses of Phenobarbitol.

The client arrived on time for her first appointment. She was unaccompanied as she would be for all subsequent appointments. Immediately after introductions were exchanged an attempt was made to secure a brief history. Mildred then complained that she felt violently ill perhaps because of a medication interaction. She requested that her appointment be rescheduled because she did not feel able to continue. Because most of the hour was left, I suggested that she lie down for a few minutes in an adjoining room and perhaps we then could try again. Mildred insisted that she must return home immediately or she would become violently ill. This was her first visit and her behavior pattern was not known to us. She was allowed to leave. An appointment was scheduled for the following week.

Mildred arrived about 35 minutes late for her next appointment. The amount of time available for an evaluation was limited. I immediately began the Bender-Gestalt. After completing the first drawing, she informed me that she had enough and would not continue. She had not slept the night before because of anxiety about today's proceeding. She then began to sob loudly and stated that these tests would confirm the fact that she is worthless and even worse, crazy. She felt that if she continued these tests she would lose her benefits and possibly be placed in an institution for the insane.

She believed that her life was totally out of control. She had been taking many tests both of the physical and mental variety over the past ten years and nothing improved her condition. She was convinced that this procedure was a total waste of time and we both had "better ways of spending our mornings."

I attempted to explain that these tests were required if she were to continue receiving any services through the foundation. In fact, not completing this evaluation could endanger her benefits. By now our time was up and I once again was forced to reschedule for the following week. Mildred said that she might kill herself between now and next Wednesday. I replied that if this came about to have someone inform us so that the time could be assigned to another client. If however, she was still with us, I definitely expected her the following Wednesday at 11:00 a.m. sharp.

After she left, I searched through her file for a clue as to a way to obtain some meaningful cooperation. She seemed to have a history of antagonistic behavior toward professionals. It was obvious that her self concept was totally diminished. My problem at this point however, was to evaluate her meaningfully, not necessarily to improve her self esteem.

It was apparent that Mildred would not return. She expressed feelings of being helpless, useless and out of control. During the week an idea occurred to me. I felt that if I gave her some power along with a sense of value she might become more cooperative.

It was customary for my secretary to call all clients the day before and remind them of their appointments. In this case, I called Mildred. Before I finished my greeting, Mildred complained about her back, head, and general condition of malaise. I decided to give Mildred a chance to improve her self esteem and perhaps view herself as an individual of worth. If I told her that I was very fond of her and that I really wanted to help her, she would have still refused since this is a line that she had heard many times before. Instead, I shared with her my supposed problem. It was very important to me and the social worker that we finish this evaluation. We did not have enough data, I explained, on brighter clients who came to the foundation. The director had informed us that if we did not complete these types of evaluations our jobs would be in danger. I told Mildred that Susan (the social worker) and I would consider it a personal favor if she would cooperate.

She appeared the next morning on time, was very cooperative and completed several tests. The following week she returned and completed the remaining tests. During the test taking there was no indication of any somatic complaints. We consistently reiterated to Mildred how much the staff appreciated her cooperation. At the end of the second session, the social worker and I presented Mildred with a small gift as a token of our appreciation. She left beaming.

Chapter 4
Uncooperativeness as Information

Merrill reminds us that the first step to treatment is diagnosis, and everything that the patient does or says is important information. Any form of uncooperativeness tells us something about the disorder that the patient has (and what kind of patient has that disorder). The tactic is to accept everything that the patient does or says in a spirit of inquiry rather than irritation, maintaining our perspectives as objective observers and not taking insults personally.

Of course, the topic of the assessment of dementia has been a major one in previous issues of *CG:*

Uncooperative Patients

George G. Merrill, MD, PhD

Uncooperative patients can be extremely frustrating to the doctor or whoever is trying to help them. While usually ignored in text-book discussions of diagnosis and treatment, they are encountered all too often in practice. So it is important for the doctor or counselor to be prepared for such encounters.

The ancient philosopher Epictetus remarked that difficulties show what a man is made of. They challenge our ingenuity, versatility and self-control. If every patient presented an orderly, rational constellation of symptoms, there would be little or no diagnostic challenge. If every patient cooperated obediently with his doctor's orders, there would be little therapeutic challenge. The uncooperative patient helps to keep us properly humble and flexible. The lack of cooperation itself may be the most important clue to our understanding of what is really happening. For example, we routinely begin our diagnostic evaluation with a statement of the patient's chief complaint, followed by an orderly account of the development of the illness, so that we can have a clear picture of why the patient has sought out our help. With a rational patient, this information can be concisely elicited in a few minutes, but we all have encountered the rambling patient who either overwhelms us with irrelevant detail or neglects to supply pertinent data on which we can base a diagnosis. This is particularly common in the older age groups. The disorganized history shows the disorganized state of the brain functions. In the most extreme cases, such as Alzheimer's disease, there may be almost complete loss of memory. With some cases of memory impairment, such as Korsakoff's syndrome, there may be pathetic attempts to compensate for the memory loss by confabulation, with fanciful stories offered to explain what cannot be remembered. With other patients there may be irrational explanations offered, as in the paranoid ones who blame their troubles on persecution by neighbors, evil spirits, or other malevolent influences felt to be victimizing them. Some patients, of course, lack the intelligence or verbal skills to organize or express any coherent account of their problem to the examining doctor. Others may have difficulty in communicating clearly because of a language barrier, speech disorder, or deafness. It is important for the doctor to formulate some opinion about the nature of the communication difficulty. Only with better understanding can difficulties be overcome.

It is important to gather information from all available sources, in order to understand any patient. Particularly this is true with the uncooperative patient. There is always someone who can supply the information the patient may be unable to recall. So it is important to learn whatever the family members, friends, employers, fellow-workers, and any doctors or therapists previously consulted may have to say. The level of education or type of job may suggest the intelligence level. The appearance of the patient, and the manner of talking, are also revealing to the observer. Answers such as "Huh?," "I don't know," or silence, must be accepted by the examiner in a spirit of inquiry rather than irritation. There is always some reason for everything a patient says or does, and the reason for an uninformative attitude may be brain damage, lack of intelligence, a language barrier, suspicion, or fear. Many elderly people, for example, fear that an examination may mean that they will be "put away" in some custodial institution. Others may never have learned English and are afraid of revealing their ignorance. In any community with some foreign-born population, it is important to have someone available to speak to the patients in their native language, both for the sake of the English-speaking examiner and for the frightened patients.

When it comes to treatment, similar problems exist. A frightened patient may not hear, an unintelligent patient may not understand. A doctor who speaks English with an accent unfamiliar to the patient may not be understood. A doctor who uses medical terms unfamiliar to the patient may confuse and frighten the patient further. The doctor who assumes that verbal orders to the patient are sufficient may overlook the fact that in many elderly patients the memory for recent events is considerably impaired, so that the patient may be incapable of remembering what he was told about medication, diet or activity. Verbal instructions should always be reinforced by written (or preferably printed) instructions to the patient and to the caretaker. Communication between any two people is like the broadcasting process on radio or television, in that both the sending and receiving equipment must be functioning, with a minimum of atmospheric disturbance, in order for the braodcast to be received clearly, and static-free. If the doctor's message-sending is not clear, or if the patient's receiving apparatus is not functioning adequately, the message may be garbled so that no real communication occurs. With elderly patients, these problems of apparent uncooperative behavior are particularly important. The doctor or counselor must be careful to avoid a reaction of impatience or resentment, remembering that any type of behavior has some underlying reason that is part of his job to discover. The treatment approach must vary, according to whether the lack of cooperation is due to lack of intelligence, lack of understanding, suspiciousness, or refusal to take orders from someone so much younger. A courteous, friendly, inquiring approach to the patient is essential if any real understanding or therapeutic progress is to occur. It may take more time, but the results are worth it.

SUMMARY

The uncooperative patient can be a frustrating problem for the doctor or counselor. Both the process of understanding and treatment can be complicated by such lack of cooperation. It is important for any doctor or counselor to remember that any behavior has a reason, and such behavior may be an important clue to diagnosis, as well as a challenge to diagnostic and therapeutic skill. With an inquiring, friendly attitude of awareness of the difficulties that elderly people face, resentment can be minimized and therapeutic progress achieved.

Chapter 5:
The Significance of Uncooperativeness
Among Retarded Elders

The developmentally disabled aged are relatively difficult to assess, owing to their lowered ability to communicate and take tests. French reports that when irritability and cantankerousness surface in these elders, it is frequently indicative of the presence of clinically significant dementia superimposed on lifelong developmental disability.

Depicted here is the case of a fortyish retarded man who became increasingly hyperactive and agitated. This case proved resistant to aversive conditioning. Finally, a CT scan verified the presence of cerebral atrophy. Conclusion: the punitive measures had only served to exacerbate the behavior.

Although the aging retarded has been a topic heretofore neglected by *CG,* a case of hyperactivity has been previously reported:

III (1) 47–55

Uncooperativeness as a Latent Indicator of Dementia Among the Mentally Retarded

Laurence French, PhD

Episodes of irritability and cantankerousness as well as confusion and language, comprehension and motor problems (agnosias and apraxias) often make those afflicted with dementia difficult to reach and seemingly uncooperative. These symptoms, however, are often more pronounced among mentally retarded clients. Dementia within this population, however, poses a clinical paradox in that while its prevalence has long been known to affect Down's Syndrome and other mentally retarded clients, these clients, especially those in the profound and severe range, defy easy detection.

Alois Alzheimer identified the pathological conditions associated with dementia some eighty years ago: "neurofibriallary tangles" and "senile plaques" in the brain. The current school of thought is that the formation of plaques and tangles are associated with the cerebral cortex and the hippocampus, those areas of the brain associated with memory and the processing of thought (Heston, 1983; Hall, 1984; Finch, 1985; Reisberg, 1983). Dementia among the mentally retarded apparently involves a greater proportion of clients, and at a younger age (onset as early as age 40).

A difficult diagnosis to make even among otherwise "normal" clients, the process of diagnosing dementia among the mentally retarded poses an even greater challenge. Here, increased client uncooperativeness offers a significant primary indicator of this afflication and could prove to be a valuable assessment tool among mentally retarded clients age 40 or older. This is especially true for clients within the profound

---

Dr. French is with Laconia State School, NH.

and severe range—those most likely to have low cognitive, and poor communication skills as well as other physical and/ or neurological handicapping conditions.

An understanding of the diagnostic classification of dementia is critical here. The DSM-III includes Alzheimer's and Pick's disease under its Axis I clinical label—Primary Degenerative Dementia. Here a distinction is made between "senile dementia" and "presenile dementia." The onset for the former is age 65 while the age of onset for the latter is before sixty-five. The DSM-III recognizes that individuals with Down's syndrome are also predisposed to Alzheimer's-like diseases. These forms of dementia, those believed to be secondary to other conditions, are coded as Multi-Farct Dementia; Other or Unspecified Substance Dementia; or Dementia due to OBS (organic brain syndrome) (Williams, 1980).

Observable features associated with dementia include deficits in memory, judgement, abstract thought, a variety of other highly cortical functions, as well as changes in personality and behavior (irritability & cantankerousness), and language/comprehension/motor coordination (Williams, 1980; Heston, 1983; Reisberg, 1983). Measurement of these features, especially among living clients, is a complex and difficult task. To date most of the knowledge concerning dementia stems from pathological research involving brain autopsies and the electron microscope. Currently, neuropsychological batteries (Halstead-Reitan and Luria-Nebraska), the electro-encephalogram (EEG), computer tomography (CT scan), and a number of medical screenings (blood sugar, serum B-12 . . .) offer the best indicators of dementia. Even then, none of these protocols are conclusive in themselves.

Features of dementia contributing to client uncooperativeness include changes in affect, ranging from anger to euphoria; increased sexual arousal, including masturbatory behavior; crying; excessive water drinking; lack, or loss, of personal management skills; aimless walking or restlessness; and a remoteness or hostile reaction when requests or demands are placed upon them. Moreover, punitive or aversive behavioral techniques are not only contra-indicated, these treatment modalities often exacerbate these associated behavioral conditions and are likely to result in adverse complications. A brief review of client "P" illustrates this phenomenon.

Client "P" was admitted to the State School in 1954 at age 16 when he became unmanageable at home. He was suspected of suffering from a dual-diagnoses of severe mental retardation and atypical psychosis. Associated features include a history of major motor seizures, kyphoscoliosis, a past history of systolic murmur, and facio, scapulo-humeral muscular dystrophy. His past behaviors included breaking windows and extreme aggression, factors which made him a prime candidate for behavioral management. Previous psychiatric evaluations had him diagnosed as possibly being paranoid. About five years ago, at age 42, mood shifts and a corresponding decrease in aggressive behaviors led to a change in the psychiatric component of his diagnosis from paranoia to possibly a bi-polar affective disorder. However, a definitive diagnosis of atypical psychosis was made until more conclusive evidence of a manic/depressive disorder could be found. In retrospect, we now realize that during this time (1981–84) Client "P"'s language showed a rapid deterioration from recognizable and socially-acceptable words and phrases to a gibberish, nonsensical utterance. Motor coordination and personal management skills deteriorated as well.

The crux of this problem surfaced, however, when a punitive approach was taken in reaction to an increase in bizarre behaviors last year. The major components of these behaviors were hyperactivity and uncooperativeness. Despite the above-mentioned indicators, a forced relaxation technique was imposed by the consulting psychologist. Here, staff, regardless of how many were needed, were required to forcefully subdue client "P" by holding him face down on the floor for as long as it took to get him to "relax." The rationale for this action was that he would soon learn that these outbursts were unacceptable. Fortunately, concerned staff challenged this rationale and requested a psychiatric and neurological evaluation. The CT scan indicated cortical atrophy while the corresponding mental status examination also substantiated a diagnosis of presenile dementia, along with possible atypical affective disorder, tardive dyskinesia, muscular dystrophy and major motor seizures.

The psychiatrist concluded that aversive behavior techniques, such as "forced relaxation," were contraindicated and if imposed could lead to serious health problems. He also noted that dementia should be the primary diagnosis superceding his historic MR diagnosis (which indicates regression from the severe to the profound range). This change is important since often treatment plans are predicated upon the client's primary diagnosis. A MR diagnosis would require, according to federal intermediate care facility (ICF/MR) regulations and State School policy, increased pressure for client "P" to "progress" developmentally. The resulting frustration would only serve to exacerbate his condition. The preferred treatment perspective for dementia is an enabling one where staff reactions are designed to minimize client stress.

REFERENCES

Finch, Caleb, E. 1985. Alzheimer's Disease, *Science,* Vol. 230, No. 4730 (December 6): 1109.

Hall, David A. 1984. *The Biomedical Basis of Gerontology.* Bristol, England: John Wright & Sons, Ltd.

Heston, Leonard, & White. June, 1983. *Dementia.* New York: W. H. Freeman & Company.

Reisberg, Barry (ed.). 1983. *Alzheimer's Disease.* New York: Free Press.

William, Janet, B. W. 1980. *Diagnostic and Statistical Manual of Mental Disorders—DSM-III* (Third Edition). Washington: American Psychiatric Association.

SECTION TWO: PSYCHOTHERAPY FOR THE UNCOOPERATIVE PATIENT

Chapter 6:
Staff Casualties
of Patient Uncooperativeness

Uncooperative patients are not the only ones who suffer. Sometimes the staff gets hurt. Although we can understand the acts of uncooperative patients, those acts cannot be condoned. Angry patients do hit, punch, bite, and scratch.

Meddaugh's retrospective study of one month in a 72 bed SNF found 30 incidents of patient physical abuse of staff, with hitting being the most frequent offense. Over an eighth of the patients (all of whom were confused) were guilty of abuse, and over a quarter of the staff were victims.

Problems with patient aggressiveness have been previously considered in *CG:*

> III (1) 51–52
> III (3) 36–39
> III (4) 78–80

as have staff/stress interactions, such as burnout:

> II (2) 39–51, 61–67

and the abuse of elders by caretakers:

> I (4) 39–52
> IV (2) 54–55

Staff Abuse
by the Nursing Home Patient

Dorothy I. Meddaugh, MS, RN

Research has documented abuse in children, spouses and the elderly population. Child abuse was reported in the literature as early as 1961. Spouse abuse has been studied for the past 20 years. Elderly abuse became evident to researchers in the early 1970's. At least one other group of persons seems to be abused: the caregivers of the elderly by the elderly institutionalized patient. As a caregiver, in an skilled nursing facility, I experienced frustration because of the lack of information and the lack of systematic research concerning this problem.

Skilled nursing facilities have become increasingly important as in-patient facilities serving the elderly in the United States. Five percent of the elderly population in the United States are residents in these facilities at any one time period. In the past, skilled nursing facilities were places where elderly persons went to die after illness prevented family members from continuing to provide care. Today, with people living longer, the advent of nuclear families, and zero population growth, older persons frequently outlive their children and need a place in which to be cared. Caregivers of elderly people must be able to give care for this population with a minimum of stress to the patient and to themselves. When physical abuse of the staff by the patient occurs, the patient may feel anxious because of loss of control and staff may be hesitant and frightened about caring for the patient. This situation produces stress and less than optimal care for these older persons.

Ms. Meddaugh is a doctoral candidate at the University of Rochester.

Funding was received from the University of Rochester School of Nursing Alumni Seed Fund and the University of Rochester Center on Aging. Special thanks go to Joyce Ferrario, PhD, RN, Mary Turner, MS, RN, and Nancy Watson, MS, RN, for their assistance with this study.

45

The purpose of the study was to determine if variables could be identified which were associated with staff abuse by the institutionalized elderly patient. Variables concerning the abuser, staff and the environment were identified for study. The specific aims of the study were: (1) to determine the frequency of staff abuse in a specified time period; (2) to identify specific demographic characteristics of the abusers; and (3) to identify specific demographic characteristics of the abused.

As stated before, documentation concerning staff abuse is limited. Primary among the small sources of research, Ochitill and Krieger (1982) reported on staff abuse in a general hospital and found that nearly all of the incidents involved patients with impaired cognitive ability. In addition, Cospito and Gift (1982) stated that the patient responsible for physically abusing staff had decreased cognitive abilities as well as increased dependency. Because of the limited documentation concerning abuse of staff by patients, a conceptual framework was formulated using literature reviewed from three other areas as well: aggressive behavior, institutionalization and abuse of children, spouses, and elders.

CONCEPTUAL FRAMEWORK

All human beings have learned aggressive behaviors (Bandura, 1973). These behaviors come out of the psycho-social, biological, and environmental experiences of the person. Some of these behaviors may include frustration (Rosenzweiz, 1977; Beck, 1976), helplessness (Storr, 1968; Halbinger, 1976) and aggression (Lions, 1972). Some of these behaviors find outlets in socially acceptable ways such as work, play or sports. Other aggressive behaviors, such as vandalism, spouse battering, and child abuse, are socially unacceptable outlets (Gelles, 1976; Rounsaville, 1978; Milner & Wimberley, 1980). When the elderly person is institutionalized, he/she still has these aggressive tendencies. Some of these persons will find new outlets which are still acceptable to society. Others will find outlets which are unacceptable to society. This study was concerned with only one unacceptable behavior: physical abuse of staff by the elderly patient.

A model was designed to clearly depict the fact that all

people have aggressive behaviors which manifest themselves in acceptable and unacceptable ways (see Figure 1). The elderly institutionalized persons, dealing with feelings of dependency and hopelessness, may experience different ways of dealing with aggressive tendencies. Some of these ways will be acceptable, others will not.

Definition of Terms

Abuse: hitting, pushing, punching, kicking, biting, scratching or other similar acts.

Staff: all persons giving direct care to the patient (registered nurses, licensed practical nurses, nurses aides).

Elderly: people aged 65 and above.

Skilled nursing facilities: an institution which provides 24-hour nursing service and has at least one registered professional nurse employed full time.

Incident reports: written report including any untoward accident or happening involving a patient or staff person.

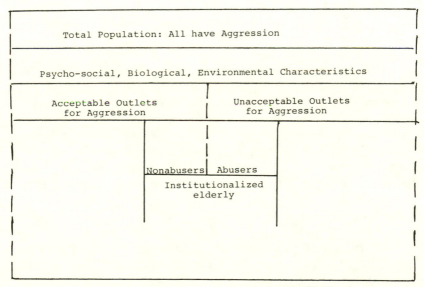

Figure 1. Model for Conceptual Framework for Staff Abuse

Research Questions

The major premise investigated was that there was physical abuse of the staff by the older patient in the skilled nursing facility. The following research questions were developed to guide the research.

1. What is the incidence of staff abuse?
2. What demographics help to identify the abuser?
3. What demographics help to identify the abused?

Research Design

The data were collected retrospectively through chart and incident report review for a three month time period. Patient characteristics of age, sex, marital status, familial supports, activity of daily living level, length of stay in facility, and visitation frequency were examined. Staff characteristics of age, education, and length of experience of working with the elderly were examined. Environmental considerations such as time of day, staff mix and other aid available at the time of the abuse were inspected.

The Setting

The investigation was carried out in a 72-bed skilled nursing facility in the northeastern United States. Physical characteristics of the skilled nursing facility included: family owned and operated; two floor patient care areas; private; located within a village; most residents came from surrounding towns; and most staff persons lived in the same village. The facility used a team nursing approach, each patient receiving care from a different caregiver on each day of a five day span.

Patients and Caregivers Studied

The patient turnover in the skilled nursing facility was a problem that had to be addressed in this study. Admissions, discharges, hospitalizations and deaths were all possibilities which had to be recognized when examining the potential sample. An isolated group of 72 patients was chosen for observation during a three month time period. These patients were studied through both incident reports and chart reviews. New admissions were not added to the sample population.

Total staff of caregivers, during the three month time period studied, numbered 97. These included full time (four days/week or more) and part time (three days/week or less) personnel.

Ethical considerations present in this study included anonymity and confidentiality of patients and staff persons. The researcher was the only person dealing with confidential information and the skilled nursing facility remained nameless in this study.

Assumptions

There were five assumptions implicit in this study. These were:

1. All major incidents of physical abuse were documented.
2. No abuse from the staff toward the patient preceeded the event.
3. All relevant aspects of the incident were included in the report.
4. The information was not biased.
5. The incidents actually occurred.

DATA ANALYSIS

This study of staff abuse by institutionalized elderly persons were carried out in a 72-bed skilled nursing facility. Data were analyzed using descriptive statistics, frequencies, means and, where appropriate, modes and medians.

Patient Information

Sixty-two (86%) of the patients were female and ten (14%) were male. The mean age was 85 years. The average length of stay in the facility was 30 months. The functional data collected from the charts on the 72 patients included mental status and activities of daily living (ADL). The four categories possible for mental status assessment were clear sensorium, minimal confusion, moderate confusion, and severe confusion/comatose. Twenty-one (29%) of the patients were rated as having clear sensorium. Fifty-one (71%) of the patients had minimal to servere confusion (more patients were moderately confused than were any other group). The four categories recorded for ADL were independent, minimal help, partial help, and complete care. Complete care was required by 38 persons (53%). All patients but one required some help in ADL's.

Social support information included marital status of the patient, number of children and other relatives and how often the patient was visited by significant others. Most of the patients in the sample were widowed (71%). Most of the patients had children (71%). Only six patients from the entire sample had no recorded supports. Patient visitation frequency indicated that patients were visited on an average of 3.4 times weekly with the mode being one time weekly. Sixty-two (86%) of the patients were non-abusive. Ten (14%) of the patients were abusive.

Staff Information

There were 97 female caregivers whose ages ranged from 16 years to 75 years. The mean age of caregivers was 32 years. The staff educational level averaged 13 years. Thirty (31%) persons worked full time and 67 (69%) worked part time. The median work experience was 14.8 months. The greatest number of staff had been employed six months or less. Twenty-six caregivers were physically abused by patients in the facility during the three month period (see Table 1).

Abuser Characteristics

There were ten abusers out of the total sample of 72 patients. Seven female residents, 11% of the 62 females, were abusers. Three male residents, 30% of the 10 males, were abusers. The abusers had an average age of 84 years.

The marital status of the residents was divided into two

TABLE 1

Number and Percent of Nursing Home Staff According to
Abuse by Patients Over a Three Month Period

Abuse by Patient	SNF Staff Studied	
	frequency	percent
Was abused	26	26.8
Was not abused	71	73.2
Total	97	100.0

categories, the widow/widower category and the "all other" category. The "all other" category included divorced, married, or never married persons. Twelve percent of the widow/widowers, or six people, were abusers. Nineteen percent, or four residents, of the "all other" category were abusers. Residents with and without children similarly abused staff (see Table 2).

Support by significant others was also examined. There were 66 residents who experienced support by significant others. Nine of the 66 (13.6%) were abusers. There were six residents who experienced no support from significant others. One of these residents (16.7%) was an abuser. Thirty-three percent of the residents who received less than weekly visits were abusers compared with 11% of the residents who received at least weekly visits.

Activities of daily living and mental status were other characteristics examined. Among those residents who needed activity of daily living assistance, 14% were abusers. There were no abusers with a clear sensorium. The rate of abuse increased as the confusion increased (see Table 2).

Abused Characteristics

The 26 staff persons were abused from one to two times. The average age of those abused was 28 years. The mean educational level of those abused was 12 years. Twelve full time staff persons and 14 part time staff persons were abused.

TABLE 2

Characteristics of Abuser and Nonabuser Skilled
Nursing Facility Patients

| Patient Characteristics | Patients by Abuse Behavior | | | | |
| | Abuser | | Nonabuser | | |
	number	rate	number	rate	Total
Sex					
male	3	30.0	7	70.0	10
female	7	11.3	55	88.7	62
Age					
< 85	6	15.8	32	84.2	38
85+	4	11.8	30	88.2	34
Marital Status					
widow/widower	6	11.8	45	88.2	51
all other	4	19.0	17	81.0	21
Children					
yes	7	13.7	44	86.2	51
no	3	14.3	18	88.0	21
All Support					
yes	9	13.6	57	86.3	66
no	1	16.7	5	83.3	6
Visitation					
> weekly	7	11.1	56	88.8	63
< weekly	3	33.3	6	66.6	9
Time in residence					
< 30 months	7	14.6	41	85.4	48
=> 30 months	3	12.5	21	87.5	24
ADL					
aid	10	14.1	61	89.0	71
no aid	0	0	1	0	1
Mental Status *					
clear	0	0	21	100.0	21
minimal confusion	4	19.0	17	81.0	21
moderate confusion	5	19.2	21	81.0	26
severe confusion	1	25.0	3	75.0	4

*p < .10

The average length of employment for those abused caregivers was 35 months. Thirty-six percent of the caregivers
under 33 years of age were abused and 14% of the caregivers
over 33 years of age were abused. There was in increased
percentage of abuse toward practical nurses (54.4%) but
there were more acts of abuse toward nurses aides (18). More
abuses occurred during the day and evening shifts. Also,
more abuses occurred to those who had been working in the
facility longer (see Table 3.)

Abuse Incidents

There were 30 recorded incidents of staff abuse during the three month period. The number of incidents ranged from one per patient to ten per patient. There were 11 (36.7%) incidents of staff abuse committed by the ten male patients. There were 19 (63.3%) incidents of staff abuse committed by the 62 female patients.

The abuse incident was investigated as to whether or not the abuser was married or had children. Eighty percent of the

TABLE 3

Characteristics of 97 Abused and Nonabused
Skilled Nursing Facility Staff

Characteristics of Nursing Staff	Staff by Abuse Experience				
	Abused		Nonabused		
	number	rate	number	rate	Total
Age **					
under 33	19	35.8	34	64.1	53
33 and over	6	14.0	37	86.0	43
missing	1				1
Education					
under 16 years	23	26.1	64	72.7	87
16 yrs. and over	1	12.5	7	87.5	8
missing	2				2
Title					
R.N.	2	7.4	25	92.6	27
L.P.N.	6	54.5	5	45.4	11
Nurses Aide	18	30.5	41	69.5	59
Duty Status *					
full time	12	41.4	17	58.6	29
part time	14	20.6	54	79.4	68
Shift worked					
day	12	35.3	22	65.0	34
evening	10	26.3	28	74.0	38
night	4	21.0	15	79.0	19
more than one	0	0.0	6	100.0	6
Work Experience					
under 16 months	11	23.4	36	76.6	47
16 months +	15	31.9	32	68.1	47
missing			3		3

*p < .10
**p < .05

staff abuse incidents were committed by the 51 widow/ widowers in the sample. Twenty percent of the staff abuse incidents were committed by the 21 "all others" in the sample. Eighty-three percent of the staff abuse incidents were committed by the 51 patients with children. Seventeen percent of the staff abuse incidents were committed by the 21 patients without children.

Patient visitation frequency was examined in the abuse incident. Of the 63 patients who were visited weekly or more, there were 80% incidents of staff abuse. Of the nine patients who were visited less than weekly, there were 20% incidents of staff abuse. All the incidents concerned patients who needed assistance in activities of daily living. All the incidents concerned patients who had some degree of confusion. The type of abuse most frequent was hitting, accounting for 57% of the cases (see Table 4).

DISCUSSION

A variety of findings surfaced from this small sample of 30 incidents of staff abuse by the elderly institutionalized patient. These findings included information pertaining to: patient activities of daily living level (ADL), sex of patient, mental status of patient, marital status, visitation frequency of significant others, type of abuse, length of facility residence, age of staff, title and education of staff, and work experience of staff.

TABLE 4

Number and Percent of Abuse Incidents by SNF Patients
Over a Three Month Period by Type of Physical Abuse

Type of Physical Abuse	Reported Incidents of Abuse	
	frequency	percent
Hitting	17	56.7
Kicking	4	13.3
Biting	2	6.7
Punching	3	10.0
Scratching	2	6.7
Unclear	1	3.3
Other	1	3.3
Total	30	100.0

Patients who needed more aid in activities of daily living caused more incidents of abuse. Male patients seemed to be more prone to abusing the staff than did female patients. Three male abusers caused 11 incidents of staff abuse or 3.6 incidents per male abuser. Seven female abusers caused 19 incidents of staff abuse or 2.7 incidents per female abuser. The abuse rate for males was 30.0; for females it was 11.3. However, a given incident of staff abuse in the facility was most likely caused by a female. All abused incidents were caused by patients who were of unclear sensorium. The "all other" marital status group were more prone to abuse as were those who had to support at all or who were visited infrequently. All of the abusers had been in the facility six months or longer.

The staff person who was abused seemed, in this sample at least, to be less educated than those not abused. Full time staff were abused twice as often as part time staff. The licensed practical nurse group was abused more often than the other two groups studied. The younger caregiver was abused more often than the older caregiver.

This type of descriptive, retrospective investigation is not without its limitations. One of these limitations was evident within this data collection: missing data (see Table 3). It was expected that the information contained on the incident reports and on the patient charts would be complete. This was not so. The investigator, therefore, was not always able to gain complete information concerning the areas of study. Possibly, if staff, patients and significant others had been interviewed, some of this information could have been obtained.

INTERPRETATION OF DATA

Dependency on others is one of the most dreaded role changes associated with old age. The aged person rebels at this new circumstance. This could help explain why the incidence of abusive behavior was higher for those patients who required much help in their normal activities of daily living. These patients could be feeling frustrated and angry because of their circumstances and because they are no longer able to release these feelings through work and leisure activities. This could also be the reason that all the incidents of abuse were caused by confused patients. The confused patient may be clinging to a former way of releasing his/her aggressive tendencies. These former ways might be totally inappropriate in the new setting. The confusion of these patients may prevent them from finding new outlets for their aggressive tendencies.

In this study, males were more prone to abusive behavior than were females. Males have traditionally been socialized to be more aggressive than females. It is possible that the institutionalized male is not as able to find new releases for his aggressive tendencies as is the institutionalized female. It is possible, however, that the female has suppressed her aggressive tendencies earlier in life and now continues that behavior.

The findings indicated that more of the abusers were patients who did not have significant others for support or who were visited infrequently. A possible reason for these patients to act out their aggressions could be lack of control over their situation. Because they experience the feelings of being alone and rejected by their family and/or significant others they may act out in socially unacceptable ways such as physically abusing the caregiver. Some of the feelings felt by the abuser could be anger, helplessness, hopelessness, and frustration over his seeming inability to control his life.

This study, though rich in description, does not indicate what was going on at the time of the abuse. It also does not indicate what the difference was between those confused and highly dependent residents who were abusers and those confused and highly dependent residents who were not abusers. It seems that the next step in research of this problem is to observe the interaction between the caregiver and the resident in the skilled nursing facility. Maybe then, we will ascertain some of the reasons behind this situation.

REFERENCES

Bandura, Albert (1973). *Aggression: A social learning analysis.* Prentice-Hall: Englewood Cliffs, New Jersey, 1–50.

Beck, Aaron T. (1976). *Cognitive therapy and the emotional disorders.* International University Press: New York, 1–100.

Cospito, Ellen & Gift, Thomas (1982). Assaultive patients in a chronic care medical facility. *Journal of Psychiatric Treatment and Evaluation, 4,* 433–436.

Gelles, Richard J. (1976). Abused wives: Why do they stay. *Journal of Marriage and Family, 38,* 659–668.

Halbinger, John D. (1976). The aged in institutions. *Dissertation Abstracts International,* Case Western Reserve University, *37,* (6-a), 3908.

Lions, John R. (1972). *Evaluation and management of the violent patient.* Charles C Thomas: Springfield, Illinois, 1–43.

Milner, Joel S. & Wimberley, Ronald C. (1980). Prediction and explanation of child abuse. *Journal of Clinical Psychology, 36,* 875–884.

Ochitill, Herbert N. & Krieger, Marilyn (1982). Violent behavior among hospitalized medical and surgical patients. *Southern Medical Journal, 75,* 151–155

Rounsaville, Bruce J. (1978). Battered wives: Barriers to identification and treatment. *American Journal of Orthopsychiatry, 48,* 487–494.

Rosenzweiz, S. (1977). Outline of a denotative definition of aggression. *Aggressive Behavior, 3,* 379–383.

Storr, Anthony (1968). *Human aggression.* Penguin Press: London, 1–60.

Chapter 7:
Psychotherapy and Self Psychology

The older psychoanalytic approach developed by Freud emphasized the need for the therapist to maintain strict analytic neutrality. Kohut emphasized the importance of object relations in self psychology. The implication that Weiner and White draw, is that the therapist must actively empathize with the patient in order to improve the latter's capacity for object relations.

The case studies are of two women in their sixties who experienced grief reactions in the wake of losses (physical attractiveness and a singing career, respectively). Weiner and White explain that the usual therapeutic approaches, based on interpretation, only secured patient uncooperativeness until the therapist came to an empathic understanding of their patients.

Previous issues of *CG* have considered psychodynamic and self psychology perspectives in geriatrics:

Uncooperative Patients or Empathic Failures? A Self Psychology Perspective

Marcella Bakur Weiner, EdD
Marjorie Taggart White, PhD

A situation in which we are listened to by another seemingly sensitive human being who is seeking to understand us and explain us to ourselves is a situation that offers us "the most crucial emotional experience for human psychological survival and growth: the attention of a selfobject milieu" (Kohut, 1984). He further points out that this milieu, via human empathy, "attempts to understand and participate in our psychological life." Empathy *per se,* the mere presence of empathy, has a beneficial, therapeutic effect both in the clinical setting and in human life, in general.

This is in contrast to the prevailing view of the 19th century where total objectivity was considered the major ideal of psychoanalysis, involving the separation of the influence of the observer from the observed, especially in relation to countertransference. However, the 20th century has brought us the profound insight into the importance of the observer upon the observed in any situation. This begins with the baby's entry into his world where human responsiveness is as essential as oxygen to the sustaining of life. Where it is provided the mother becomes the internalized good selfobject; where there is a deficiency, it is, hopefully, repaired in the therapeutic situation where the therapist ultimately becomes the good selfobject to a patient whose impaired self indicates the deficiencies of his original selfobjects. If the therapist accepts this

Dr. Weiner is a psychotherapist in private practice and Adj. Professor, Fordham University Graduate School of Social Service. Dr. White is a psychoanalyst in private practice and founder and director of the Seminar in Self Psychology.

requirement, it means that he/she will have to empathically try to understand where the adult patient failed to receive the emotional oxygen he/she needed to develop a healthy self and how a strange adult, the therapist, can begin to fulfill this void.

TO EMPATHIZE OR NOT TO EMPATHIZE

Most therapists, in our view, would prefer to think of themselves as empathic even though empathy might be modified to no gratification. On the other hand, the patient either may seem in danger of insatiably wanting more and more gratification, owing to original deprivation, or conversely, needs to learn to tolerate frustration because he was given too much. In either of these cases, the therapist can be in a quandary as to how much and what kind of, if any, empathy he should communicate to the patient. However, leaving aside these usual indecisive soliloquies of the therapist who is less committed to empathy than to exploring the unconscious, let us consider the therapist who is really concerned about empathic self psychology.

Here is a supervisory case of a therapist experienced in and disposed toward being empathic who is treating a very depressed woman. She had previously been a successful singer in night clubs and in Broadway musicals but had to give this up because of her advanced age and because of endless conflicts with her managers. Now, at age 63, she had come to treatment in connection with a possible chance to do a television talk show and was overwhelmed with a depressive conviction that she would lose this chance as she had lost so many others. Here is a replay of the therapeutic interchange around this issue.

Therapist: I can understand how anxious you must be about losing this really big chance to get into a different field but, after all, you have shown yourself to be such an experienced performer, right at the top.
Patient: Yeah. Thanks a lot. (Pause) You don't seem to realize that it can't ever be the same. Who needs this?
Therapist: Well, I understand that this talk show is not the

same as being on Broadway. Still, you sang in night clubs for quite a while before you made Broadway.

Patient: You remember that I sang, and I remember that I sang, and for a singer there is nothing in the world like singing. I suppose it's like a dancer dancing. Just talking words, no matter how many people are listening, is not the same.

Therapist: Well, I can understand what you're saying, but still we have to be realistic about the chances we get.

The patient missed the next session and then took a "vacation" from therapy because of pressing work problems. She did not return for another year, but the fact that she did return indicates that she felt some empathy from the therapist. What she later explained and he came to realize was that he did not and perhaps could not empathize with what it means to be a singer not to be able to sing any more for a living. As she put it very movingly, "it is like taking the voice from a bird."

This kind of empathy requires a "feeling into" the other person. We can try to imagine what it is like for a singer not to be able to sing any more for her living but, if we are not a singer, we cannot imagine the expressive loss and the blow to one's self-esteem. Still, if we can imagine what it would be like to lose a precious skill we have, e.g., for the therapist it would have to be talking and hearing, we can then imagine what the loss and rage would be for a singer. Here we are not concerned with the economic or career loss but rather the experiential, creative loss that would go back to the nuclear self of childhood. To tune in on this would be real empathy.

THE CRUCIAL PROBLEM OF GRATIFICATION

There is a hint in the supervisee's response to the patient, before she left treatment for a year, of his understandable concern that she could spoil the realistic chance she had to resuscitate her career with a television show. Yet, the patient felt misunderstood enough to leave treatment for a year, with the implication that the therapist's focus on reality triggered narcissistic rage in the bereaved singer. We use the word "bereaved," advisedly, because we are confronting the fact that the loss of a self-fulfilling talent such as singing can be as great a loss as the failure of a love relationship including the death of the loved one. So we are, as therapists, entering into an area of very profound feelings when an important talent is frustrated or even completely blocked, e.g., when a dancer is so injured that she can no longer dance (Weiner & White, 1982).

But what does gratification have to do with the therapist's overconcern with a reality situation which would then block his capacity to empathize with a major loss which his patient is suffering? Here we have to go back into history on what was supposed to have been regarded as the proper scientific stance of the psychoanalyst. In this version, the therapist is to retain his stance of neutrality, be reality-oriented and use his skills much as the surgeon would whose aim would be the successful performing of an operation.

Yet, we may ask, is empathy *per se* defined as beneficial and therapeutic, a gratification? Two dictionary definitions, (Thorndike, 1956; Reader's Digest, 1967) state that to "gratify" is to "give pleasure or satisfaction to" and both suggest "satisfy" as a synonym. The more recent (1967) defines "satisfy" as follows: "to supply fully with what is desired, expected or needed." The earlier one (1956) defines "satisfy" as "give enough to" and also "put an end to (needs, wants, etc.)." We are, perhaps, being pedantic in trying to clarify what gratification and satisfaction are held to mean, in common parlance and yet the very word, "gratification," evokes guilt, anxiety and defensiveness among psychoanalysts and psychotherapists.

EMPATHY AND INTERNALIZATION

If a trained mental health practitioner is willing to try to help a patient reduce his/her anxiety, low self-esteem and feelings of helplessness and abandonment by love objects, there has to be at least relief from pain and some restored hope for the future. This is true for patients at every age! This relief and hope can be seen as fulfilling minimal needs in living and, according to the dictionaries, the therapist would consequently be gratifying the patient. That there is implicit gratification in the therapist's constancy, reliability and his perception of the patient's unique identity, seems obvious. Thus, "gratification can be seen as a necessary part of how the therapist offers himself to the patient as the potentially good selfobject the patient has never had. This internalization of the therapist as the good selfobject the patient never had is necessary for the patient's arrested development to proceed" (White and Weiner, in press).

Yet, despite the above, a form of "maturity morality" may be used unthinkingly, but nonetheless destructively, in the therapist-patient relationship. For the therapist to assume that the patient "naturally" understands and accepts the therapist's maturity morality and to demand an accounting if the patient's reactions do not jive with the therapist's expectations can too often leave the patient feeling totally misunderstood and uncared about. It can also propel the patient out the door permanently, leaving the therapist convinced that the patient was "untreatable"—i.e., "uncooperative" because he/she had certainly done nothing to precipitate the patient's leaving.

Failures in empathy are experienced by many patients much as they were experienced by the child early in life: as outrages perpetuated upon a self seeking an open responsive environment as one seeks fresh air to suck into a living organism. Ruptures with the human environment are felt as threats to the self.

MARIE: THE CASE OF AN EMPATHIC RUPTURE

A supervisee provided a moving example of an empathic rupture. He had first met the patient, Marie, at a meeting at a senior center where he had given a talk. She had approached him afterwards, expressing her appreciation of his presentation. She then added that she was quite dissatisfied with the therapist she had been seeing for two years and indicated that she would like to see him. The supervisee was aware that there might be complex feelings connected with her wish to change therapists so he said he could arrange a consultation to explore the advisability of their working together. He also thanked her for her appreciative remarks about his talk.

When Marie came in for the consultation, she confirmed the supervisee's impression of her as an attractive woman in her mid-sixties—tall, slim, and intelligent looking. It turned out that she was married, with two grown daughters and three grandchildren. She still worked part-time in advertising where she appeared to be doing a competent job. He did not notice her physical limitation—a slight limp from a childhood bout with polio—until she mentioned having had polio. She also explained that she had a problem buying shoes since only special types, though sold in regular shoe stores, could fit her.

Obviously, taking much pride in her appearance, she reported spending considerable time in seeking and getting shoes which were also attractive and matched her outfits. She explained that she loved getting "dressed up" to go to work and put much effort into this.

At this point, the supervisee found himself wondering how appropriate a discussion of her shopping habits was in a consultation about whether to start treatment with him. However, since whe was talking about shopping for something related to a childhood illness that undoubtedly was traumatic, he decided not to interrupt. Marie went on to say that recently a favorite type of shoe for her had been taken off the market and replaced by updated styles which were difficult for her to wear. She had complained about this to her previous therapist, Dr. J. He had, with a slightly superior air, asked her why she didn't have the customary "special" shoes made for her.

Marie told the supervisee she had reacted with horror to this suggestion, saying to her previous therapist: "But I spent years as a child, wearing just that kind of awful-looking shoe and waiting for kids to ask me why I was wearing those 'old-lady' shoes. Or sometimes, they would just point and whisper. When they laughed, it was the worst! I still shudder when I think of all those awful years and how hard I fought to learn to buy regular shoes and to look like everybody else!"

The supervisee found himself very moved by Marie's eloquent description of the painful humiliation she had suffered because of her childhood handicap and her struggles to overcome it. He wondered how her previous therapist had tried to compensate or apologize for his insensitive suggestion. He did not have to wonder long because Marie told him.

"If only you weren't so vain!" her previous therapist had

said, shaking his head disapprovingly. At this point, Marie said she started to cry. It was not so much the painful memories of the past as it was the great disappointment she felt in him at not understanding her feelings.

"I suddenly felt as though I were miles away from him, as though he had never been there for me at all. I began to think of other comments like this. Suddenly, my anger welled up and I thought, 'What am I doing in therapy with a man like this? He doesn't really understand what I'm saying at all!' "

Marie looked at the supervisee, sighed and said, "It was then I was sure I had to change. I left the session and called him the next day to say I simply could not continue. When he asked me to come in to discuss it, I said I had been thinking about it for quite a while and would prefer not to. And that was that."

The supervisee said, "I can understand how you felt." He was relieved that he had not been somewhat unempathic in asking her what the purpose of a shoe-shopping discussion was, given the pressure of time in an initial consultation. He particularly realized that it was not so much the previous therapist's failure to tune in on her childhood suffering as it was his flagrant disapproval of her "vanity" that had made Marie feel completely uncared about. To imply that she was pathologically narcissistic in her natural desires to be admired and thought attractive "like everyone" was to deny her inborn right and need to be exhibitionistic, as if her childhood handicap had permanently deprived her of the appreciative mirroring she so desperately needed to compensate for her childhood traumas. Fortunately, now in her mid-sixties, Marie's childhood experiences seemed to have given her enough healthy mirroring and ambition to strive to overcome her handicap and make the most of her assets. Yet her self-esteem was sufficiently vulnerable, not only because of the polio trauma but also because her father had suddenly disappeared on her in an impetuous separation from her mother.

A "Maturity Morality" Therapist vs. "Vanity"

Her expectations for an empathic father figure to be there for her reliably, with sensitive attunement, had been severely undermined by the disappearance of her father and had, inevitably, made it difficult for her to trust other men to be dependably loving. She had come to treatment mainly over this problem, with an unconscious conviction that her child-hood problems had driven her father away and continued to discourage other men. Long-term marital problems seemed to give further evidence of this. She was easily convinced that what she experienced as the remoteness and insensitivity to her feelings from Dr. J. was all she, poor maimed Marie, could ever expect until she became what Dr. J. and other "acceptable" men expected her to be, whatever mysterious way of being that was. But Dr. J.'s gauche "maturity moral-ity" in criticizing her for her "vanity," when she was strug-gling so hard to compensate for her handicap, made her suddenly realize that the gap in understanding between this therapist and her feelings was too huge. Whatever he wanted to develop her into, she wouldn't want to be anyway!

She had found the supervisee's discussion of later-age prob-lems at the senior center meeting sufficiently appealing to overcome her cynicism about ever finding a therapist she could trust to be even minimally sensitive. In the consulta-tion, she also found him empathic enough to start seeing him on a regular basis.

A most delicate listening and imagining task is called for in a consultation where a patient has become disillusioned in a pre-vious therapist. The empathic approach requires that we strive to stay solidly on the side of the patient and not let ourselves be tempted to "understand" why the previous therapist might have had difficulties. The supervisee veered toward a confron-tational approach in wondering whether he should question all the talk about shoe-shopping. If he had not stopped to think of what a lame leg from polio could do to her feeling of desirabil-ity as a woman, he might have disillusioned her as much as Dr. J. did, perhaps permanently. If we always try to think of how what we say will feel from the patient's standpoint, this effort at empathy will rarely mislead us.

EMPATHY AND SELF PSYCHOLOGY

Self psychologists are often accused of near-sightedness, i.e., they only look at the self state of a patient and nothing more. While this is generally true and follows along with

Kohut's (1977) exciting concept of the supraordinate self as being the ultimate touchstone of our existence, nevertheless Kohut certainly leaves the door open for object relations problems, particularly in his expansive approach to the oedipal experience as having the normal potential of being joyous rather than an experience burdening one with guilt for the rest of his days.

But it is crucial, for diagnostic and treatment-process reasons, to consider the various possibilities of where a patient is at and where a patient wants to go (if indeed, the patient has any concrete ideas about this!). Where a patient consciously wants to go and seems capable of going may vary appreciably from where the therapist may realistically believe that the patient has the capacity to go. If we are still locked into Freudian drive theory or "realistic" ego psychology, then we may feel pressured to think of the patient as a "neurotic" with a blazing or submerged oedipal problem. Or we may think that the patient has had an accrual of pre-oedipal developmental deficits which hamper normal ego development, including object relations. In either case, the self of the patient is not considered by the therapist any more than the patient probably considers it! In our experience, the patient who comes in with an urgent "I" problem forces us to consider the "I" even though we may, with our maturity morality objections to flaunting narcissism, object to so much emphasis on the self as opposed to object relations.

From our years of clinical practice, while being trained in traditional approaches, we have found the use of the self psychology model, with its emphasis on the empathic stance, to be a most useful one. Empathy, as used in this model, is the so-far-as-we-know unique human capacity to feel oneself into another's psychological life and to attempt to understand it and, on the basis of that understanding, to attempt to participate in it. From the therapist's position, the attempt will be to try to participate in the other's psychological life as a development-enhancing selfobject, to compensate for the inadequacies of the parental selfobject. In the larger sense, beyond therapy, empathy is what everyone needs in trying to feel and understand the psychological lives of those close to us or whom we need to understand professionally if we are to work effectively with them.

Where empathic failures take place, this has often been interpreted as a "negative transference" reaction. It is our feeling that where this occurs, this is a revival of an old injury to the cohesion of the self, proving to the child how unattuned his/her selfobjects were to his feelings. What the child needed (and did not get) from his/her selfobjects, in terms of mirroring his ambitions and achievements and in terms of being an omnipotent ideal, become guidelines for how the psychotherapist can become a good selfobject to the patient, a second chance or a "new edition" of selfobject experience (Kohut, 1977). The working through of selfobject transference thus involves picking up where the original selfobject left off.

What the psychotherapist is offering to the patient is a second chance to believe in and then to internalize a good, reliable selfobject which the patient never had. This may become a major area of conflict in the treatment and one of the most disheartening countertransference feelings for the therapist, i.e., that he/she has not had any effect at all! However, if the therapist reviews where the patient was at at the start of treatment, and where the patient is now, quite often the therapist may be very heartened at how much progress has actually occurred.

THE REWARDS OF SELF PSYCHOLOGY

Self psychology, we have found, helps deal with impasses which have produced therapeutic failures where there might have been successes. This approach calls upon the therapist continually to ponder the impact of his/her intervention and to explore this impact if it seems to have distanced the patient. The therapist is called upon to set aside interpretive approaches that make the patient feel misunderstood, often triggering dangerous regression. This involves the therapist's admission that his interpretation or sometimes what is experienced as a moralistic attitude is off the track in the sense that it makes the patient feel indicted rather than empathically understood. For the older patient, it may be the *first time* in his/her life that this is given to him/her. For the therapist, at any age, the process of self psychology can be a searching and regenerative process as well.

REFERENCES

Kohut, H. *The Restoration of the Self.* New York: International Universities Press, Inc. 1977.

Kohut, H. *How Does Analysis Cure?* Chicago: The University of Chicago Press. 1984.

White, M. and Weiner, M.B. *The Theory and Practice of Self Psychology.* New York: Brunner/Mazel, Inc. (In press, 1985).

Weiner, M.B. and White, M.T. Depression as the search for the lost self. *Psychotherapy: Theory, Research and Practice.* Vol. 19, #4, 491–499. Winter, 1982.

Chapter 8:
Cognitive-Behavior Therapy
and Uncooperativeness

In many ways, the opposite of the empathic approach to uncooperative-ness, is for the therapist to respond with more structure, clarity and self-defined tasks. If this is done in such a way as to increase the patient's sense of control over his/her environment, or sense of self-worth, the therapeutic results are positive.

Silven and Gallagher have found uncooperativeness to be prevalent in depressed elders. They present the case of a 65 year old woman in cognitive-behavior therapy. Results were minimal, largely because of the patient's failure to do the required homework. She interrupted the cognitive therapy sessions which her own agenda: that her own situation was hopeless. The therapists developed techniques and cues to get the patient back on the track. Success came when one of her cognitions about her role as caregiver of an aged mother was discussed in the open, and any evidence of doing homework was acknowledged and rewarded.

Previous issues of *CG* have contained articles and clinical comments on cognitive therapy or training:

I (3) 45–52
II (3) 15–23
III (3) 44–45
III (4) 17–34
IV (1) 48–50

The specific issue of the importance of "homework" has been addressed previously:

III (3) 61–63

Resistance in Cognitive-Behavioral Therapy: A Case Study

David Silven, PhD
Dolores Gallagher, PhD

Recent findings (Zeiss, Breckenridge, Gallagher, Silven, Schmit, & Thompson, 1985) indicate that client noncooperativeness is characteristic of a sizable proportion of depressed elders receiving short-term outpatient psychotherapy. That is, even among those clients whose depressive symptoms remit by the end of therapy, pervasive failure to cooperate with the treatment procedures appears to be an extremely common phenomenon. In psychodynamic therapy, resistance to treatment might be regarded by the therapist as a natural and perhaps even welcome opportunity to examine the client's dysfunctional behavior and internal dynamics. In more structured cognitive-behavioral approaches, however, client noncooperativeness would seem to limit the client's opportunity to practice and thereby learn the cognitive and behavioral coping skills which the therapy attempts to provide. The following is a description of the course of short-term cognitive-behavioral therapy with a minimally cooperative elderly depressed client. This client's noncooperativeness presented serious challenges to the establishment of a collaborative therapeutic relationship.

Mrs. A is a 65-year-old widowed black female with a 9th grade education who sought therapy with the complaint of feeling overburdened and irritable as the caregiver for her 87-year-old mother. She also felt guilty about the adequacy of

Drs. Silven and Gallagher are with the Center for the Study of Psychotherapy and Aging, Veterans Administration Medical Center, Palo Alto, California.
This study was supported primarily by grant #5 TO1 MH17621-03 from the National Institute of Mental Health.

her care for her mother. Mrs. A stated that her distress had gotten progressively worse during the past year, which she associated with the progressive deterioration of her mother's mental functioning and the increase in the mother's demand-ingness and dependency. She reported no history of depres-sion or other emotional problems prior to the onset of the current distress. At intake, Mrs. A was diagnosed as clinically depressed with no other significant psychopathology present.

The client was treated with a total of 17 individual sessions of cognitive-behavioral therapy (Beck, Rush, Shaw, & Emery, 1979), wherein the primary focus is on modification of the client's maladaptive ways of viewing him/herself and the world. Therapy was initiated with a through overview of the cognitive-behavioral rationale and procedures, including the reading of an article describing the therapy (Beck & Greenberg, 1974). Such initial orientation to the cognitive-behavioral therapy process seemed strongly indicated with the client who, like many older persons unacquainted with psychotherapy, con-veyed the rather vague expectation of this therapy as a place to feel better by "getting things out in the open."

Despite persistent efforts by the therapist to induce appro-priate expectations and behavioral compliance with these ex-pectations, the client was minimally successful throughout the therapy in carrying out the tasks prescribed by the therapist. She failed to do most homework assignments, including read-ings, recording of thoughts, feelings, and behaviors, and ex-perimentation with new behaviors intended to test the validity of her thoughts. During the sessions, she tended to interrupt the therapist in his attempts to systematically focus on mal-adaptive thoughts and behaviors, giving detailed accounts of her mother's troublesome behavior during the previous week. Mrs. A appeared determined to convince herself and the ther-apist that her situation as a caregiver was unchangeable and unmanageable.

Several adaptations in the treatment were successfully im-plemented to enhance the client's cooperativeness and active participation in therapy. An agenda was explicitly agreed upon at the beginning of each session and was written in bold letters on a blackboard for reference during the session when-ever the client seemed tangential in focus. A hand-signal was used by the therapist, with considerable success, to reorient the client whenever she began wandering from the topic at hand. The client agreed to take notes of important points during each session, which were reviewed at the beginning of the following session as a way of maintaining continuity of focus from one session to the next. At the end of each session, the client was asked to give a summary of the session in her own words, which allowed the therapist to correct any misconceptions and clarify when the client's understanding of material was incomplete. Finally, audiotapes of sessions were given to the client to take home, providing a basis for further review and consolidation of the main points of the sessions.

A turning point in therapy seemed to occur with the successful challenging of an important cognition related to being a caregiver. The client clung to the notion that taking better care of her own needs was selfish and would only distract her from her responsibilities as a caregiver, thereby reducing her adequacy as a caregiver even further. The therapist engaged her in considering the possibility that taking care of herself might enable her to be a more effective care provider for her mother and for others as well. This was a novel alternative to her original view and seemed logical enough for her to test out as an hypothesis. During the remainder of therapy, she became increasingly willing to "try experiments" such as limited practice of daily progressive muscle relaxation, and planning some pleasurable activities (Lewinsohn, Munoz, Youngren, & Zeiss, 1978) into her daily schedule. Through careful examination of the evidence, she came to recognize that the quality of care she provided for her mother was not sacrificed and was perhaps improved in some respects, as a result of her taking better care of herself.

The client's notion that her situation was unmanageable was gradually challenged by her increasing sense of efficacy in being able to make small changes in her daily life (Meichenbaum & Gilmore, 1982). Although Mrs. A continued to be sporadic in her completion of homework, evidence of *any* attempts to carry out assignments were acknowledged and reinforced by the therapist, as were the client's increasingly frequent reports of self-initiated changes. Examples of such changes included locking the door to her bedroom for one hour each night to keep her mother from interrupting her privacy during that time, and talking rationally to herself in stressful situations in order to feel more in control of her response.

Therapy terminated four sessions after the client decided, upon the recommendation of her family physician, to place her mother in a nearby nursing home. More time to review therapy gains and to plan for future application of the cognitive-behavioral skills clearly would have been preferable. However, the client's highly irregular attendance after placement of the mother seemed to be her way of letting the therapist know that she wanted to terminate. Mrs. A was interviewed at the time of therapy termination by an independent evaluator and was found to be no longer symptomatic of depression.

This case illustrates the potential value of building a large degree of structure and well-defined tasks into therapy with older clients. Through consistent encouragement and reinforcement of efforts and successes by even highly resistant clients such as the one in this case, the resulting enhancement in sense of efficacy and self-control can provide the impetus for meaningful change and improved mental health.

REFERENCES

Beck, A. T., & Greenberg, R. (1974). *Coping with depression.* New York: Institute for Rational Living.

Beck, A. T., Rush, A. J., Shaw, B. F., & Emery, G. (1979). *Cognitive therapy of depression.* New York: Guilford Press.

Lewinsohn, P. M., Munoz, R. F., Youngren, M. A., & Zeiss, A. M. (1978). *Control your depression.* Englewood Cliffs, N. J.: Prentice-Hall.

Meichenbaum, D., & Gilmore, J. B. (1982). Resistance from a cognitive-behavioral perspective. In P. Wachtel (Ed.), *Resistance: Psychodynamic and behavioral approaches.* New York: Plenum Press.

Zeiss, A. M., Breckenridge, J. S., Gallagher, D., Silven, D., Schmit, T., & Thompson, L. W. (1985, November). Client cooperation and the outcome of psychotherapy for depression in the elderly. Paper presented at meeting of the Gerontological Society of America, New Orleans.

Chapter 9:
Meeting the Patient More Than Halfway

Shute also notes the prevalence of uncooperativeness in depressed elders. One frequent problem is the first and most important step of getting them into the office for evaluation and treatment. Shute presents a case of a 78 year old man, who refused to come in for psychotherapy, but agreed to meet the psychologist for breakfast at a delicatessen. This provided the opportunity for some behavior and social assessment. Continued breakfast meetings provided an environment for successful cognitive psychotherapy.

Other articles and clinical comments on depression management have appeared in previous issues of *CG:*

I (1) 83–84, 97–98
I (3) 15–37
I (4) 71–73
II (1) 3–29, 45–53
III (1) 25–45
IV (2) 19–30, 38–40, 46–48

Psychotherapy of Reluctant, Depressed Elders

George E. Shute, PhD

Frequently, a depressed elder is referred for psychotherapy but is unwilling to come to the therapist's office for treatment. Consequently, not only are they reluctant to ask for help, they are unwilling to make much effort to take advantage of it if it is offered.

Existing models for therapy for depression in the elderly have been shown to be very effective treatments (e.g., Gallagher & Thompson, 1981) but such studies have only been reported in the usual clinical settings.

This case will illustrate how effective a traditional therapy can be for depression in a reluctant, aged client when delivered in a very non-traditional manner.

Mr. L. is 78 years old, was divorced three years ago, lives alone in an apartment, and has multiple medical problems including diabetes, hypertension, variable peripheral vascular circulation and macular degeneration. Additionally, a consistent clinical impression was that he was seriously depressed.

Although he had frequently sought medical assistance for his physical conditions, adherence to prescribed treatment was questionable. Further, there was a long history of refusal to consider any type of psychological assistance.

Scheduling a home visit for the initial contact, we planned to complete a multiple-focused assessment to determine his degree of medication compliance, his nutritional status, whether he was actually depressed and to assess his general life-style and the amount of social support available. Mr. L. would only agree to the diagnostic interview for the affective disorder. Rational explanation of the reasons for the additional assessment was of no use. Nor would he agree to participate in

---

Dr. Shute is with Indiana State University.

anything labeled or referred to as counseling or psychotherapy. He did however, agree to meet for breakfast and that proved to be the key.

At the first such meeting, at a delicatessen close to his apartment, a behavioral assessment was initiated. Observing what Mr. L. ate and using the occasion to talk about food provided substantial data as to his usual nutritional intake. Watching him interact with other "regulars" and the proprietors in the deli demonstrated his social skills and when walking back to his apartment, his interactions with neighborhood residents and shopkeepers clearly revealed a substantial portion of his social network and quality of those interactions. Medications compliance was assessed by direct question.

Over the next several months, breakfast meetings every two to three weeks provided an excellent environment for cognitive psychotherapy for his depression. For example, Mr. L. had been consuming large amounts of sugared soft drinks on the assumption that all sugar free soft drinks tasted bad. A simple experiment of trying one of the new drinks after breakfast successfully challenged the assumption and resulted in the immediate dietary change desired. Modeling of appropriate food selection was possible. Reality issues such as decline is physical health, divorce and loss of friends were dealt with effectively using cognitive therapy. Cognitive distortions and erroneous, underlying assumptions were identified and modified. He learned to deal with new stressors more effectively so that although his overall level of depressive symptomology improved only slightly, he was able to handle increasing blindness without becoming more depressed. Behaviorally, Mr. L. reinitiated contact with estranged family members and became more assertive instead of passive/aggressive with medical personnel.

An initial concern about doing therapy in a public setting was not supported. It may be that cognitive therapy may sound like conversation to others in the area. In this case, significant issues were worked with and the setting seemed more to facilitate such exploration than inhibit it.

The major factor in the success of this approach seemed to be a willingness to meet a reluctant elder on his own grounds, both literally and figuratively. With the environment providing the psychological link between the idea of friends meeting for breakfast to the reality of a client-psychologist meeting to do psychotherapy, it was possible to engage a very distressed elder in the process of his own mental self-care.

REFERENCE

Gallagher, D., & Thompson, L. W. (1981). *Depression in the elderly: A behavioral treatment manual.* Ethel Percy Andrus Gerontology Center: Los Angeles, CA.

Chapter 10:
Intergenerational Psychotherapy for Uncooperative Patients

About a fifth of American elders live with younger relatives. Even in cases where they do not live together, the involvement of the younger generation in a case may be essential for effective intervention.

Jones and Flickinger argue that it is only when a family can openly discuss what is "owed" by who to whom that it can begin to deal with the crisis posed by a dependent elder. The case is presented of an 88 year old father and the daughter on whom he had grown dependent. It was only after both sides were able to air their long term grievances with each other that they were able to come to a cooperative a realistic solution to his physical needs.

Although the contextual approach of Boszormenyi-Nagy may seem somewhat innovative, at least in its application to multi-generational therapy, the effectiveness (and necessity) of the family context for geriatric intervention has long been demonstrated in many previous issues of *CG:*

I (1) 69–95
I (2) 59–67
I (4) 53–67, 75–78
II (1) 61–62
II (3) 15–23
III (2) 5–17, 37–38
III (3) 3–15
III (4) 17–34
IV (2) 19–30

Contextual Family Therapy for Families With an Impaired Elderly Member: A Case Study

Scott Jones, MA
Mary Ann Flickinger, BA

In recent years, Shanas (1979a, 1979b, 1980) has done much to dispel the once commonly held myth that the elderly become more and more alienated from thier families and die lonely deaths in inhumane institutions. Families tend to provide much support for elderly members and continue to fulfill this "familial duty" throughout the elder's life-span. Meeting this responsibility is often difficult and draining emotionally, if not materially. Circumstances sometimes combine to make the task even more difficult. Brubaker and Brubaker (1981) noted that approximately 20% of the elderly live with relatives and the potential for greater levels of stress for all parties concerned is increased. Regardless of living arrangements, the "aging family" often undergoes changes and challenges specific to dealing with a frail elderly member. The question of how best to provide therapeutic services to such families is beginning to receive the attention it deserves in the professional literature.

TRADITIONAL GROUP APPROACHES

In the past five years a large number of studies have been published on group work intervention to aid families with

The authors are doctoral students, Department of Psychology, Miami University, Oxford, OH. They gratefully acknowledge a critique of an earlier draft of this paper by M. Powell Lawton and two anonymous reviewers.

elderly members (e.g., Cohen, 1983; Hartford & Parsons, 1982; Hausman, 1979; Lazarus, Stafford, Cooper, Cohler, & Dysken, 1981; Silverman & Brahce, 1979). These models for intervention share several basic themes: (a) an educational component in which participants learn more about the emotional, physiological, and other deficits and changes associated with aging; (b) an informational component outlining community resources and available support services; (c) development of peer support in the group to share common problems and stresses; (d) an emphasis on decision-making regarding how group members could more appropriately manage their responsibility to an elderly relative. All the groups were short term (6 to 10 sessions), semistructured, and did not involve any conjoint work with the elderly relatives. That is, it was hoped group members would be more able to accept the decline of elderly relatives (usually parents) and deal with this fact on a more objective level (similar, in part, to Blenkner's [1965] notion of "filial maturity"). All studies reported moderate success in helping members by reducing stress through sharing it with others and in facilitating decision-making regarding their responsibility vis-à-vis the elderly relative.

Schmidt (1980) stated that the problems associated with dealing with an impaired elderly parent are actually of two orders—those problems caused by the "age structure" of elderly parent and adult offspring, and those problems due to long-standing conflict. The former difficulty refers to situations created by competing demands often experienced by middle-aged or young-old (Neugarten & Hagestad, 1976) offspring who attempt to provide resources to their children, plan for their own retirement, etc., *and* meet their responsibility to a very aged parent as well. Schmidt noted sheer fatigue as a prevalent problem for persons in this situation. Long-standing conflicts are generally due to unresolved developmental issues on the part of the adult offspring. For example, some persons are never able to adequately separate from a domineering parent. These persons may continue to live close by or with a parent, overly depend on them for emotional or other support, and be unable to accept the decline of such a parent who has remained so powerful in their lives. According to Schmidt, long-standing conflicts are a greater barrier to achieving filial maturity than are conflicts related to the ages of the "child" and parent.

The group work approaches discussed above tend to focus on age structure aspects of the stress experienced by families dealing with elderly relatives. They attempt to help group participants find solutions to the real challenges of providing adequate care for elderly family members without over-whelming other members of the family. That adult offspring are committed to meeting their responsibilities to elderly parents is well supported. There is no widespread abandonment of the elderly (Shanas, 1979b, 1980). Cohen (1983) suggested that middle-aged persons are in a developmental era in which interdependence is highly valued. Thus, maintaining elderly members as part of the family is also valued. Given the family's desire to act responsibly toward elderly members and the inherent difficulties presented by this situation as a function of historical conflict and the age structure of family, a therapeutic approach is required that allows the family to deal with *both* of these issues.

Boszormenyi-Nagy (Boszormenyi-Nagy & Spark, 1973; Boszormenyi-Nagy & Ulrich, 1981) developed a conceptual model and therapy approach that deals directly with familial issues accounting for the need for interdependence and the difficulty in maintaining such interdependence. This alternative therapy approach, which attempts to understand and alleviate the long-standing conflicts within families and aid in the process of gaining "filial maturity," is the contextual family therapy model developed by Boszormenyi-Nagy.

CONTEXTUAL FAMILY THERAPY

Contextual family therapy (Boszormenyi-Nagy & Ulrich, 1980) is a comprehensive relational approach that focuses on the entire relational family system. The contextual orientation is based on the assumption that the leverage of all psycho-therapeutic interventions is anchored in relational determinants. These determinants may be considered through four interlocking dimensions: facts, psychology or what happens within the person, transactions or power alignments, and relational ethics.

The first dimension of relational determinants is "facts" or historical truths about the family. These may include births, deaths, injuries, illnesses, perceived obligations, and cultural identity. The second dimension is that of "psychology" or what happens within the individual person in the family. A variety of facts exists for each family member as well as for the family as a whole. This dimension addresses how the family members feel about these facts, their attitudes and reactions. The third dimension is transactions or power alignments. These include "transactions" or exchanges between family members over time. Individual family members may establish coalitions. For example, mother and child may function as a unit "against" father, forming a power alignment. The last dimension, relational ethics, Nagy considered the cornerstone of contextual therapy. Such ethics are concerned with the balance of equitable fairness among family members. "Equitable fairness" entails "the long-term presentation of an oscillating balance among family members, whereby the basic interests of each are taken into account by the others" (Boszormenyi-Nagy & Ulrich, 1981, p. 160). Furthermore, Boszormenyi-Nagy described his contextual approach as embracing any intervention model which takes into account the equitable balance of fairness in the family.

Issues of "entitlement" or indebtedness among family members are present whether this "entitlement" is acknowledged or not. Essentially, relationships become trustworthy to the degree that the relationships permit family members to face the issue of who "owes" whom. Grounded in relational ethics, an action or consideration toward the payment of the debt or toward realization of an "entitlement" is seen as a fundamental move toward building trust or "health." The family is strengthened by moves toward trustworthiness and weakened by moves away from it. Moves toward trustworthy relatedness are termed rejunctive; moves away from such relatedness are dysjunctive. When one family member contributes to the balance by regarding and supporting the interests of other family members he/she acquires "merit."

In the contextual approach, the concept of "ledger" refers to an accumulation of the accounts of what has been given and what is owed. The ledger involves two components: (a) the debts or entitlements dictated by "legacy," and (b) the accumulation of merit through contributions to the welfare of other family members. "Legacy" encompasses the specific configuration of expectations that originate from rootedness within a given family system and the resulting impingement on the generations of offspring. Thus, "entitlements" may be what is due a family member as a parent in combination with what that family member has come to merit. The parent-child relationship is asymmetrical in that the child's "entitlement" naturally exceeds its indebtedness. This balance gradually shifts as the child moves toward adulthood and increasing interpersonal power (i.e., as he/she becomes increasingly accountable for taking action to preserve the ledger balance).

At times, the "legacy" brought by an individual into his/her family of procreation is such that the therapeutic approach may involve the individual's family of origin. Framo (1981) developed such an approach wherein further understanding and exploration of early relational balances is achieved through conjoint family therapy involving the individual, parents, siblings, etc. It is held that patterns of behavior will emerge in the family of origin that the individual has transferred to his/her family of procreation and actively maintains. This approach allows the individual to "balance accounts" with the persons with whom these relational patterns were originally created or enacted. It strives to decrease the need to "finish" old relational business within new relationships, freeing the individual to start anew in these relationships. (Boszormenyi-Nagy developed many new terms to describe the aspects of the intergenerational family context. While these new terms may first appear as unnecessary jargon, they actually describe relational aspects of the family not easily discussed using terminology originally devised to describe families.)

A fundamental difference between the contextual approach described above and the group therapy discussed earlier is that contextual therapy attempts to enable the family to discuss relational issues that have been difficult or impossible to discuss previously. The group work approach offers a setting in which common relational problems across families may be discussed, but it typically does not engender this discussion within families. This is a critical difference in that the contextual approach posits it is more likely that benefits will accrue to all family members by engaging in this trust-evoking work. It allows the opportunity to understand together the manner in which long-standing problems or issues make the current situation (i.e., care of an impaired elder) more difficult.

In the following case example, an aging family was able to accomplish significant rejunctive movement in the course of one extended conjoint meeting. Due to circumstances of the case (i.e., the physical impairments of one of the participants, the urgent need for immediate intervention, unavailability of other family members), only a father-daughter dyad was seen in therapy. Ordinarily, several generations would be included in such treatment if available and willing to participate.

> Mr. W., an 88-year-old retired farmer, had lived alone for the past five years since his wife was placed in a nearby nursing home. He was almost totally deaf due to injuries he suffererd in a heavy equipment accident in the 1940s. The accident crushed both of his inner ears and almost killed him. Otherwise, he was in remarkably good physical condition and still owned and managed two rental properties for the extra income. He had been alienated from his later middle-aged daughter, Mrs. Y., when Mrs. W. was moved to a nursing home several years previously. Mrs. W. needed skilled nursing care but her husband was unwilling to let her go to the home. Mrs. Y took legal action to have her mother placed in the home. Mrs. Y related that she and her father had been unable to talk without arguing since this incident and she was becoming afraid he might physically attack her.
>
> Mr. W. lived independently with little assistance since his wife had left. With only minimal aid from his daughter and grandniece, he had provided for his own care although Mrs. Y. stated she wanted to help her father more, but he would not allow it. Mr. W.'s constant companion was a small dog who walked with him on his many excursions (he no longer drove). The adaptation Mr. W. had been able to maintain was lost when his pet wandered from his home and was accidentally killed by a passing car. Mr. W. became confused, in-

sisted someone had murdered his dog, and refused to let it be buried. Relatives attempted to bury the dog for him, but when they arrived he threatened them with bodily harm.

Mr. W. was probated through the local court and, at this point, the first author was called to complete a psychological evaluation of him. Except for his suspicions regarding the death of his pet, Mr. W. was found to be intact and competent. He clearly had many sensory and other deficits (e.g., poor dentation, hygiene, malnourished). The court was willing to discontinue the probation process if equitable arrangements could be made to provide care for Mr. W. Mrs. Y., who had begun the probation, was contacted and she stated a willingness to meet with her father and the therapist to discuss Mr. W.'s current problems.

A conjoint meeting revealed that Mr. W. had never forgiven Mrs. Y. for instigating her mother's move to the home. When Mrs. Y. was able to share that, while it upset her too, she saw no alternative, Mr. W. was willing to further share his anger and sadness over the incident. After much "bartering," Mr. W. agreed to have Meals-On-Wheels bring him lunch every day and to let Mrs. Y. assist him in cleaning, cooking, etc., on a several-times-per-week basis. Mrs. Y. expressed relief at being able to again have some relationship with her father. No further therapeutic contact was initiated by the family.

A follow-up interview 15 months later with Mrs. Y. revealed that the relationship between Mrs. Y. and her father had improved greatly following the conjoint session. Mrs. Y. saw her father on a daily basis and assisted him with household chores. Mr. W. became progressively weaker due to a malignancy, however, and died approximately one year after the therapy contact. Mrs. Y. reported he was "stubborn and strong-willed" until his death. During his illness Mr. W. moved to the same nursing home where Mrs. W. had lived for many years, but he only stayed a week. He apparently could not give up the independence that he had maintained all his life. He died a short time afterward in a medical hospital.

DISCUSSION AND THEORETICAL EXPLICATION

This case is illustrative of life-long relational balances or patterns in the family. Mr. W. had always been an independent person and expected to take care of himself and his family. According to the physicians who treated him, it was a "miracle" he even survived his mid-life injuries much less continued to do hard manual labor. As he aged, it became increasingly difficult for him to allow others, even his own daughter, to aid him. He saw Mrs. Y.'s attempts to provide care for him and his wife as, in some ways, "disloyal" to his legacy of independence. This left Mrs. Y. unable to repay her debts to him, or to begin to deal with his physical decline, because he persisted in maintaining he could always manage alone. His increasing emotional, social, and physiological isolation eventuated in his appearing as if he was brain damaged (Ernst, Beran, Safford, & Kleinhauz, 1978), although he was intact under clinical inquiry.

The relatively short therapeutic contact appears to have been effective because it involved both parent and offspring in a discussion not just of Mr. W's physical needs, but both of their feelings regarding their relationship over time. Similarly, Framo (1982) stated that after having done individual and family psychotherapy for many years, he believed one conjoint family therapy contact may be more valuable therapeutically than "an entire course in one of the other therapies" (p. 169). Mrs. Y. was able to share her sadness at angering her father over the nursing home placement of Mrs. W. She also made it clear she wanted to help her father in whatever way was necessary. Although he was less able to discuss his feelings, his willingness to allow Mrs. Y. to become actively involved in assisting him suggests he too was willing to see her position. Individual psychotherapy would have been nearly impossible with Mr. W. due to his severe hearing loss. In fact, Mrs. Y. was instrumental in aiding the therapist in communicating with Mr. W. His speech had become idiosyncratic as a result of not being able to clearly hear his own voice, and while Mrs. Y. did not speak for her father, assisting him seemed to bring them closer together. It appears the conjoint work started a process which continued during the last year of

Mr. W.'s life. Mrs. Y., at least, felt her relationship to Mr. W. had improved remarkably by the time of his death.

In terms of measuring this therapy outcome, we only have self-report data, and then only for one of the involved persons. There is still much debate about what contitutes an adequate measure of family therapy outcome and Boszormenyi-Nagy is less than clear in addressing this issue regarding contextual family therapy. Regardless, a stronger case could have been made for the efficacy of the contextual family approach in the present case if Mr. W. could have been interviewed regarding his feelings about the outcome. Extended follow-up of the surviving family members might profitably explore the effects of the interventions made in the described therapy contact.

In conclusion, it could be argued that in many cases the elder is so incoherent or uncommunicative that contextual work would be futile. However, even the more disorganized, organically impaired persons have periods of emotional and cognitive clarity. Conjoint meetings reduce the isolation considered by Ernst et al. (1978) to be so devastating to mental functioning. However, there are cases in which the contextual approach could not be practically applied. Some families are so alienated that conjoint or concurrent work would be impossible and group or individual psychotherapy could be employed. Occasionally, there is only one surviving member of a family, in which case the contextual model could be useful as a means to structure individual psychotherapy interventions. Second, the group work approach may profitably be used in conjunction with the approach discussed here. Many persons are poorly informed of normal age changes and the group format appears to be a useful way to disseminate information and provide support among members. Perhaps families could meet in a group setting to discuss naturally relevant issues. Last, the importance of dealing with intergenerational relational issues during the elder's lifetime should be a primary therapeutic goal. While family members can address one another, the possibility of balancing accounts or ledgers is always open. Once a member dies, these balances may perhaps only be dealt with in generations to follow. In this particular case, the family had a final year to work on these accounts. Contextual family theory suggests that a lasting benefit was thereby obtained for younger or future generations in this family because they are, in a sense, freer to build their account in the family without being negatively involved in the older generation's relational issues.

This suggestive clinical example is the basis for empirical research that should further explore the applicability of the contextual family therapy model. Of particular usefulness would be research on the conditions under which the contextual/intergenerational model has a higher likelihood of therapeutic benefit than group or individual models of intervention. Such research should also explore the utility of meaningfully combining these approaches in some clinical situations and should study those patient or family characteristics which contraindicate the present model in therapy with impaired elderly persons.

REFERENCES

Blenkner, M. (1969). The normal dependencies of aging. In R. A. Kalish (Ed.), *The dependencies of old people* (pp. 27–37). Detroit: Institute of Gerontology, University of Michigan-Wayne State University.

Boszormenyi-Nagy, I., & Spark, G. M. (1973). *Invisible loyalties.* Cambridge, MA: Harper & Row.

Boszormenyi-Nagy, I., & Ulrich, D. (1981). Contextual family therapy. In A. S. Gurman & D. P. Kniskern (Eds.), *Handbook of family therapy* (pp. 159–186). New York: Brunner/Mazel.

Brubaker, T. H., & Brubaker, E. (1981). Adult child and elderly parent household. Issues in stress for theory and practice. *Alternative Lifestyles, 4,* 242–256.

Cohen, P. M. (1983). A group approach for working with families of the elderly. *Gerontologist, 23,* 248–250.

Cohler, B. J. (1983). Autonomy and interdependence in the family of adulthood: A psychological perspective. *Gerontologist, 23,* 33–39.

Ernst, P., Geran, B., Safford, F., & Kleinhauz, M. (1978). Isolation and the symptoms of chronic brain syndrome. *Gerontologist, 18,* 468–473.

Framo, J. L. (1981). The interaction of marital therapy with sessions with family of origin. In A. S. Gurman & D. P. Kniskern (Eds.), *Handbook of family therapy* (pp. 133–157). New York: Brunner/Mazel.

Framo, J. L. (1982). *Explorations in marital and family therapy: Selected papers of James L. Framo.* New York: Springer Publishing Company.

Gurman, A. S., & Kniskern, D. P. (Eds.). (1981). *Handbook of family therapy.* New York: Brunner/Mazel.

Hartford, M. E., & Parsons, R. (1982). Groups with relatives of dependent older adults. *Gerontologist, 22,* 394–398.

Hausman, C. P. (1970). Short-term counseling groups for people with elderly parents. *Gerontologist, 19,* 102–107.

Lazarus, L. W., Stafford, B., Cooper, K., Cohler, B., & Dysken, M. (1981). A pilot study of an Alzheimer patient's relatives discussion group. *Gerontologist, 21,* 353–358.

Neugarten, B., & Hagestad, G. O. (1975). Age and the life course. In R. H. Binstock & E. Shanas (Eds.), *Handbook of aging and the social sciences* (pp. 35–55). New York: Van Nostrand Reinhold Co.

Schmidt, M. G. (1980). Failing parents, aging children. *Journal of Gerontological Social Work, 2,* 259–268.

Shanas, E. (1979a). Social myth as hypothesis: The case of the family relations of old people. *Gerontologist, 19,* 3–9.

Shanas, E. (1979b). The family as a social support system in old age. *Gerontologist, 19,* 169–174.

Shanas, E. (1980). Older people and their families: The new pioneers. *Journal of Marriage and the Family, 42,* 9–15.

Silverman, A. G., & Brahce, C. I. (1979). As parents grow older: An intervention model. *Journal of Gerontological Social Work, 2,* 77–85.

SECTION THREE:
CASE MANAGEMENT FOR UNCOOPERATIVENESS

Chapter 11:
Handling Uncooperativeness
In a Deinstitutionalized Patient

Bemak uses the case of a 68 year old man to illustrate a four fold procedure for dealing with uncooperativeness. First, emphasize the patient's safety and sense of control in the here and now. Second, delicately introduce emotional content. Third, make the transition to the present. Fourth, develop empathy with the feelings underlying uncooperativeness.

101

A Four Step Clinical Intervention Model: Treatment With the Resistant Patient

Fred Bemak, EdD

The following is an outline for a model of clinical intervention with the uncooperative patient based on a brief case study. The four step model is presented utilizing therapeutic interventions to illustrate each phase of treatment. The patient was a 68 year old male residing in a nursing home who had refused to leave his room for six months. He had been at the nursing home for 3 years following a two decade period of institutionalization in a state hospital. The Massachusetts Department of Mental Health was concerned about his increasing unwillingness to speak with nursing home staff, mental health professionals, and case managers as well as his progressive physical and emotional withdrawal. Subsequently I was requested to provide a clinical consultation.

STAGE ONE: SAFETY

The aim in beginning to establish rapport with a resistant and withdrawn patient is to introduce a climate of safety. This was done by focusing on concrete non-threatening aspects of his reality. Thus speaking about his roommates, the posters on his wall over his bed, his television set with a name tag on it, and a stack of letters on his dresser produced a communication and interaction about his external world. The opening

Dr. Bemak is Assistant Professor, Department of Human Services and Professional Leadership, College of Education and Human Services, University of Wisconsin–Oshkosh.

dialogue in this first stage also enhanced a sense of personal control on the part of the patient by emphasizing areas of conversation about which he had full knowledge and the consultant did not. Two byproducts of this were allowing the patient to assess his ability to trust the clinical consultant and to gain a sense of security by speaking about "uncharged" topics.

STAGE TWO: INTRODUCTION OF EMOTIONAL CONTENT

The second stage of treatment with a resistant patient involves the introduction of emotionally laden content. This must be done delicately in order not to threaten the patient who may already be frightened and established in noncompliant interactional patterns. In this stage it is important to begin to include closer intimate non verbal interaction such as increased eye contact, slightly closer physical proximity to the patient (i.e., leaning forward or pulling one's chair closer), and a small modification in the tone of voice to indicate the introduction of new communication patterns. The second stage provides an outlet for emotional cartharsis on a topic area which the patient would like to address rather than a direct focus on the presenting problems of resistance.

The patient introduced his anger and frustration at being institutionalized for 20 years. This was encouraged to facilitate the expression of emotional content. There was support for the patient to continue to express these feelings in order to foster a level of comfort on an affective level.

STAGE THREE: THE BRIDGE TO PRESENT

There is point in time where past ventilations become counterproductive for an uncooperative patient. It is at this time when the clinician must move into the third stage and begin to bridge the patients' feelings to present issues. Emotions which the patient expressed in stage two must be maintained in the transition to stage three. Hence the patient was asked if he was angry at anyone or anything presently.

It is important to recognize at this stage that the movement to the present is not immediate. The third stage only initiates a phase of the transitional process that provides linkage between underlying emotions and the patient's uncooperativeness. Thus when the patient began talking about being unable to do carpentry and his feelings of increased physical and emotional pain it was an important tie with emotional content.

It can be seen that the clinician must be extremely patient and understanding with the noncooperative individual. The patient must be allowed to move at a pace which he is capable and willing, especially in light of the extent of his resistance level.

STAGE FOUR: BEHIND THE UNCOOPERATIVENESS

In the fourth stage one must almost create a unity with the patient about his feelings. It is a sense of empathy which provides a perspective of joining with the patient so that the roles of clinician–patient have merged to become two looking out at the world as one.

The first three stages created an environment of understanding, trust, empathy, and safety for the patient. Furthermore, there was an emotional catharsis. In being permitted to move on his own emotional pathway the patient achieved a sense of self confidence and alliance with the clinician. There was increased psychological movement by the patient towards his own emotional truth and rationale. Simultaneously the patient was talking with the clinical consultant about that truth which contributed to his rejection of other individuals. It is at this time that the clinician may facilitate the process of treatment by encouraging the patient to speak more directly about his cognitive understanding of the origin of the uncooperativeness and the affect accompanying these perceptions. This may be done with more direct questions or comments about the specific presenting problem.

When questioned the patient willingly explained his dilemma which was twofold. He had received a walker five months prior to our meeting due to increased difficulty in walking. Due to the clutter of trays, wheelchairs, tables, and medicine carts in the nursing home hallway it was nearly impossible for him to maneuver through this chaos. He had tried speaking to staff about his frustration but felt unheard. The second problem related to a case manager who had resigned five months previously. The patient and the case manager had enjoyed community activities and recreational activities together on a bi-monthly basis. Before the case manager left he promised the patient a special trip to the zoo. For five months the patient had been waiting for the case manager with growing disappointment and anger. He had inquired about the staff member during those several months without gaining a sense of understanding or resolution.

There are numerous cases of uncooperative patients. I have continued to find this four step model and to be highly effective in working with the problem of resistance.

Chapter 12:
Managing Medication Non-Compliance

Wood focuses on non-compliance in a case of unipolar depression in a 70 year old woman. The key to compliance was to remove both the stigma about taking mood altering drugs and guilt about the disorder. Tactics included educating the patient about the appropriateness of the medication and positive side effects, in addition to getting the family's support. Also helpful was structured daily activity schedules which gave her a feeling of small victories in mastering the environment.

The lesson to be learned from this case is that uncooperativeness does not have to be seen as a monolithic and unalterable personality trait, but a series of separate habits which can be modified little by little, and success in making the patient cooperative in one area facilitates success in other areas.

The topic of medication non-compliance has been dealt with several times in *CG:*

III (3) 17–22
IV (1) 3–15

Uncooperative Behavior in Unipolar Depression: Managing Medication Non-Compliance

Ava Wood, RPN

Uncooperative behavior in psychogeriatric clients is of particular concern to therapists because of increased vulnerability associated with the aging process. The reasons for lack of cooperation vary widely, but include such factors as fear of loss of independence, impaired cognitive and reasoning ability, sabotage by significant others, or a personal bias against psychiatry and stereotyped images of aging and mental illness. When the uncooperative behavior includes non-compliance with medication, it is important that these factors be examined and dealt with immediately to ensure amelioration of symptoms before the elderly person's health and lifestyle are seriously affected.

The following case history illustrates the management of uncooperative behavior in a case of unipolar depression, highlighting the management of medication non-compliance:

> Mrs. T. was a 70 year old married woman experiencing her second episode of unipolar depression in five years. Her symptoms met the DSM III criteria for major depression and included preoccupation with thoughts about her own unworthiness and the futility of her future, and mild paranoid ideation about church members who she felt had turned against her. Her husband was impatient at her inability to "snap out of it"

The author is with the Community Psychogeriatric Program, Alberta Social Services and Community Health, Edmonton, Alberta, Canada.

and refused involvement with community nurse visits. Her children, although supportive and concerned, were in disagreement as to the exact nature of her problem and the most appropriate course of action. Mrs. T felt guilty about the effect of her depression on the family and was quite anxious about an upcoming family holiday out of the country, which they were reluctant to cancel for financial reasons. The referral to Mental Health Services was made by a granddaughter with Mrs. T's grudging consent.

A consulting psychiatrist prescribed a tricyclic antidepressant to be gradually increased over a 4 week period; however, Mrs. T was resistive to taking the medication, using it sporadically and contrary to the prescribed regimen. She was also resistive to continued family physician follow up for her borderline diabetes. She expressed ideas that the treatment and community nurse visits were futile and resisted recommencing activities. The family were advised to cancel the trip but decided to continue their plans for her inclusion.

Mrs. T showed no alteration in depression symptoms during her two week holiday, but this had the positive effect of convincing her family that she had required formal treatment, and assuring their cooperation. To ensure medication compliance, Mrs. T was seen at home twice weekly for the first three weeks and then once weekly until she was cooperating fully with treatment. During these visits she was encouraged to discuss her feelings about the overall treatment plan, including any concerns about the medication. Mrs. T revealed that she did not believe medication could cure such severe symptoms as hers and that in addition to her own perception of stigma about having to take "nerve pills," her husband viewed psychotropic medication as "dope" to which she could easily become addicted. In addition, one of her daughters was a firm believer in natural vitamins and organic preparations and had advised her mother against the use of harmful "chemicals."

To remove the social stigma and alleviate guilt feelings about her illness, in order to make treatment more acceptable to herself and family, she was encouraged to view her depression in the same light as any other biological condition of insidious onset requiring medical treatment. Because she was diabetic, this condition was used repeatedly to illustrate examples of people who at times required medication to bring the condition under control but who were not considered drug addicts. She was given concrete examples of other elderly clients with similar symptoms who had shown a positive response to antidepressant therapy. Teaching was done on each visit about the action of the medication, and because one of her main complaints was her constant fatigue from insomnia, emphasis was put on some of the positive side effects such as sedation, which she was told to expect if she took the medication as prescribed. Because her sleep, appetite and energy level showed improvement before her depressed affect and thought content, and because she developed a dry mouth, she used the medication erractically at first, stopping it for two or three days or undermedicating in the belief that it wasn't working.

Family support was enlisted to encourage compliance in two ways: first, by checking with children prior to each visit for indications of progress, which were then linked to the medication and reinforced by the therapist as obvious signs to her family that she was getting better. Secondly, the family were educated to encourage her compliance despite mild side effects such as dry mouth by handling them as positive occurences indicating effective therapeutic blood levels of the medication.

After two months of regular chemotherapy, Mrs. T. felt enough improvement to try stopping the anti-depressant. She was advised by the possible adverse outcome but given control of the decision, and the brief relapse in symptoms served to reinforce her continued cooperation with medication.

To overcome Mrs. T's feelings of uselessness and resistance to recommencing activities, she was given a daily schedule to simple tasks and her daughters were enlisted to work beside her to initiate these activities, including a weekly outing. It was necessary to review this schedule during each weekly visit as her subjective impression for several months continued that she was accomplishing little unless confronted with the evidence of what she'd done.

Mrs. T's negative attitude to check-up with her physician was influenced by her belief that she was "too old" and partly by the same daughter who supported natural vitamin therapy. However, after repeated educating about the effects of untreated medical conditions on overall health, she was seen and treated with antibiotics for a bladder infection, and resumed a diabetic diet for elevated blood sugars. Each small measure of success served to increase Mrs. T's cooperation to the overall treatment program. 18 months later, she is asymptomatic on a small maintenance dose of tricylic antidepressant, maintains a busy lifestyle and visits have been reduced to every two to three months by the community nurse.

As illustrated by the case history, the therapist must show considerable perseverance with the elderly uncooperative client. Treatment generally requires more concrete and directive approaches, and sessions should be more repetitive than is usual with a younger clientele. Many uncooperative clients never show the same degree of positive response demonstrated by Mrs. T, but her case does reflect that persistence in eliciting compliance in one area can lead to cooperation with other aspects of treatment.

Chapter 13:
Milieu Therapy
for the Dementia Patient

Thornbury reviews the disruptive behaviors of dementia patients as catastrophic reactions to their decreasing ability to cope with increasingly unfavorable environments. The message for caregivers is two-fold. First, don't take such hostile behavior personally. Second, reduce the incidence of such behaviors by attempting to make the patient's environment less confusing, less threatening.

The management of dementia cases has been a frequent topic in previous issue of *CG:*

I (1) 45–49, 87–95
I (2) 77–81
I (3) 3–7, 9–13, 93–94
III (3) 36–39

Milieu therapy has also been covered:

IV (1) 83–84

Catastrophic Reactions

Julia M. Thornbury, RN, MSN

Disruptive and unexpected behavior outbursts in dementia patients are perplexing and frightening. These outbursts may be extreme with physical violence, or they may be less severe, characterized by irritability and crying. Family, dementia patients and caregivers are all victims of what is known as "catastrophic reaction."

Catastrophic reaction is the behavioral outcome of cognitive disorganization when the dementia patient is incapable of meeting demands of the situation (Goldstein, 1952). Marked by extreme anxiety, the resulting disordered behavior renders the patient helpless to control emotional or physical responses. Generally, the disordered behaviors are thought to be both unavoidable and unpredictable, and thus are distressing and exhausting (Mace & Rabins, 1981).

Catastrophic reactions occur in varying degrees of intensity. Minor episodes are usually represented by brief, verbal expressions of anger or signs of restless tension (Goldstein, 1952). This disturbing behavior may appear to be willful, in which the dementia patient is being obstinate or overemotional (Mace & Rabins, 1981). On the other hand, catastrophic reactions can be uncontrollably violent and potentially harmful to caregivers. Fear and frustration from cognitive disorganization generate anger and hostility causing the patient to strike out indiscriminately. Often family and caregivers respond with these same emotions of fear and anger, which then escalates the emotionally charged situation (Bartol, 1979).

While causes of the disorganized and sometimes explosive

Ms. Thornbury is currently a doctoral student, University of Rochester School of Nursing. A portion of this paper was presented at the annual meeting of the Gerontological Society of America, New Orleans, November, 1985. Research was supported in part by NRSA: Division of Nursing Predoctoral fellowship, #1F31 NUD 5872-01.

115

behaviors are puzzling, there are antecedent commonalities. Individuals with dementia may be unable to communicate their needs to others, or to understand themselves what others are trying to communicate. Thus, emotional outbursts from the demented individual may be seen as an attempt to communicate unmet needs (Gwythe & Blazer, 1984). Further, the failure to understand when confronted with a task or question may result in frustration or combative behavior (Bartol, 1979). For example, questioning the demented person during a interview may present unrealistic cognitive demands that trigger a catastrophic reaction.

To compound expressive or receptive communication deficits, misinterpretation of the environment, or of persons in that environment, may evoke intense feelings of fear. Surprising the demented person by approaching suddenly, or touching patients when they are unaware someone is nearby may evoke extreme reactions. These difficult behaviors are more frequent when routines are changed, or the demented person is in new surroundings. Often, a visit to the doctor or even to a friend's home, will be overwhelming to the dementia patient and precipitate inappropriate emotional reactions. A new caregiver, or frequent changes in caregivers, is generally disruptive to the demented person resulting in cognitive disorganization.

The discrepancy between the demands made on the dementia patient and the individual's capabilities often precipitate catastrophic reactions (Goldstein, 1952). For example, expecting demented persons to comply with complex directions may be beyond their abilities. Brushing teeth and getting dressed are very complex tasks for a cognitively compromised person. Resistance to the command "take your bath" is one of the more common signals that the task is simply beyond the cognitive resources of the demented person. It is this margin between ability and demands that may cause inappropriate behaviors.

Superimposed on the divergence between demands and individual abilities is an increased vulnerability to cognitive disorganization when the demented person is tired or overstimulated (Bartol, 1979). Moreover, the pressures to hurry individuals with dementia while they are slowly and deliberately attempting to cope with demands, will almost certainly increase the potential for intensifying inner tension, perhaps escalating into an explosive outburst (Goldstein, 1952).

Catastrophic reactions may be prevented, or at least modified in severity in dementia patients (Mace & Rabins, 1981). Interventions to prevent these outbursts of uncontrollable behaviors parallel the causes. Caregivers and families can learn to simplify daily activities by subdividing complex tasks into manageable components, while allowing plenty of time for patients to accomplish their goals. Maintaining a consistent, predictable routine with familiar caregivers is essential. This continuity minimizes the stress on an already compromised mind.

Sensitivity to non-verbal behaviors may provide clues to an impending outburst. Increased motor activity, raised pitch and volume in the voice, tightened jaws and lips, and a flushed face all may be signals that the person is becoming overwhelmed (Bartol, 1979). Searching for the source of distress and preparing to intervene, while maintaining a calm response, may modify the reaction.

In summary, catastrophic reactions are not willful behaviors, but instead signal that the margin is too great between demands on dementia patients and their cognitive resources. Feelings of distress may linger in the dementia patient long after the precipitant is forgotten (Mace & Rabins, 1981). Learning to avoid or at least modify these disruptive behaviors is a major goal in caring for persons with dementia.

REFERENCES

Bartol, M. A. (1979). Nonverbal communication in patients with Alzheimer's disease. *Journal of Gerontological Nursing, 5*, (4), 21–31.

Goldstein, K. (1952). The effect of brain damage on the personality. *Psychiatry, 4*, 245–260.

Gwythe, L. P. & Blazer, M. (1984). Family therapy and the dementia patient. *American Family Physician, 3*, 149–156.

Mace, N. L. & Rabins, P. V. (1981). *The 36 Hour Day*. Baltimore: Johns Hopkins Press.

Chapter 14:
Behavioral Management for Uncooperativeness

Proulx and Campbell use the case of a 78 year old paranoid male to illustrate behavioral management of an outpatient. The key tactic here was to use the caregiver wife as the behavioral observer. It was she who had to be trained how to chart baselines and relate them to antecedents and consequences. Later she was instructed in how to reinforce her husband's appropriate behaviors. The results were significant drops in confused and paranoid behaviors.

Behavior therapy has been one of the most frequent topics in previous issues of *CG:*

Management of paranoia was specifically discussed in:

The Management of Apparent "Paranoid" Behaviour In a Patient With Multi-Infarct Dementia

Guy B. Proulx, PhD
Kenneth B. Campbell, PhD

This article describes the use of a behavioural management programme for the assessment of underlying causes of an unusual case of "paranoid," disoriented conduct. Subsequently, a controlled programme of intervention was undertaken to reduce the incidence of disruptive behaviour. The procedures used in this programme are similar to those described by Hussian and Davis (1985). Thus, the object of the behavioural management programme was initially to identify observable behaviour that was targeted for change. Baseline assessment of the type, frequency and duration of inappropriate behaviour was then made. Intervention procedures were subsequently brought into play through the manipulation of environmental reinforcement contingencies. Throughout the programme, data were continuously collected to provide an objective means of determining the efficacity of the treatment programme. The case involves a 78 year old male, TB, who over the course of the past 4 years, began to show increasingly abnormal behaviour.

PREVIOUS HISTORY

TB has had a record of memory loss that has become worse over time. Recently, he has displayed very frightful,

Dr. Proulx is Director of Neuropsychological Services, Elisabeth Bruyère Health Centre, Ottawa, Canada; Dr. Campbell is Associate Professor, School of Psychology, University of Ottawa, Canada.

paranoid-like behaviour. In particular, he was obsessed by things breaking and a fear of fire. He would, at times, strike himself on the head and pitch stones at people passing in the street. Although he has had paranoid ideations, there were no hallucinations. There was little indication of depression. Within the past year, he was admitted into the psychiatry ward of a local, acute-care hospital where he was administered antipsychotic medication. He was subsequently referred to the Neurology department where an EEG and CT examinations were carried out. The former showed a mild generalized non-specific disturbance of cerebral activity over the temporal lobes. The latter suggested an advanced degree of cerebral atrophy involving mainly the lateral ventricles and basal subarachnoid spaces. There were relatively large patches of infarctions on the left posterior temporal and right anterior and mid-temporal regions. The patient was then transferred to the Geriatric Day Hospital of the Elisabeth Bruyère Health Centre (EBHC). Here he was referred for neuropsychological evaluation.

TB had no insight into his deficits. Because he could not maintain an appropriate level of mental effort, a full neuropsychological evaluation was not possible. A brief mental status evaluation was therefore performed. TB was particulary disoriented towards the concept of time. On simple tests of attention, he did quite well. He could, for example, repeat up to 5 numbers forward. When tasks were slightly more difficult and demanded more concentrated effort (such as counting up by 3s or counting backwards), his performance deteriorated remarkably. The manner in which errors were made revealed a noteworthy pattern. Initially he did well, but soon appeared to forget the "rules" of the task. He therefore clearly understood the instructions but could not retain the information. These observations were reinforced on all tests of verbal and non-verbal memory. Although he could "register" information (repetition, simple auditory comprehension), he could not retain any of the information even after a few seconds delay. He did well on long-term, remote memory, but needed cues to assist him retrieving and accessing the information. Language functions—repetition, naming, auditory comprehension, reading and writing—were well preserved. There were some mild difficulties with apraxia but results were well within normal limits for his age. Tests of perceptual and constructional abilities were normal as were tests of stereognosis and finger tapping. It was concluded that TB had severe anterograde amnesia and was incapable of learning anything new except through rote learning. These results were consistent with large, multiple bilateral infarctions of the temporal lobes.

Given TB's lasting disturbances of memory, disorientation, apathy and agitation, it was decided to place him on a behavioural management program in an attempt to alleviate his "paranoid" tendencies. At home, his wife was asked to analyse problematic behaviours in terms of their relationships to other events. She was asked to keep a daily log of events antecedent to the inappropriate behaviour and the consequent behaviours (those that follow it). The goal of this assessment was to provide information about the frequency and the duration of the "paranoid"-like behaviours as well as the nature of the variables that maintain it. We suspected that many of these inappropriate behaviours were a consequence of the severe anterograde amnesia and subsequent confusion.

BEHAVIOURAL MANAGEMENT PROGRAMME

In order to obtain a meaningful and quantitative understanding of TB's disorder, it was decided to place him on a controlled behavioural management programme. Since he was an outpatient (coming to the Health Centre only once or twice a week), his wife was used as the "behavioural observer." She was initially supplied with an ABC (antecedent-behaviour-consequence) chart. She was asked to indicate when problematic behaviour occurred and to provide a description of the behaviour in as much detail as possible. Furthermore, she was asked to recall precisely what events preceded the behaviour and following it, the consequential behaviour. The first week of observation served as a "baseline" period. As such, no intervention was attempted. A sample of the first week's ABC is illustrated in Table 1. Over this baseline period, 30 "confused-paranoid" behaviour patterns were noted (see Figure 1). A number of features of the ABC chart were striking. First, his wife was able to

TABLE 1: BASELINE OBSERVATION PERIOD

DATE	TIME	ANTECEDENT BEHAVIOUR	PROBLEM BEHAVIOUR	CONSEQUENTIAL BEHAVIOUR
25-09	0930	Got up from sleep	Said: "What did I have for breakfast? "Where are my pants?" "Were you painting?" "I must be dreaming"	Had breakfast
	1430	TB came back from getting a haircut	"I should get more of these quarters (\$0 25) for the bus. (He had 20). "Where could I get them?"	Had a rest
27-09	1000	Got up from sleep	"Are you my wife? Where is your mother?"	Wife: "She passed away years ago." TB: "Oh yes, that is right."
	1500	Came home from bank. Trimmed flowers and hedge	"Are there any sparks in the flowers?" "Will the blossoms fly up?" Will they do damage?"	Had a rest
28-09	0800	Got up from sleep	"Where are my pants? Did you take my stuff away?"	Wife: "What stuff?" TB: "My money. I haven't a cent You leave me broke. Come on Give me my money."
28-09	1530	Got up from sleeping	"What goes up to the roof? (Removes cobble stones.) "The things are up to the ceiling."	Wife: "What things?" TB: "I don't know. There's a name for it. Come look it over. See the paper on the bed." Wife: "There isn't any paper." (TB goes into bedroom)
29-09	0730	Got up from sleep	"Give me my money. I left it in my pocket. You'll be a nice mess. They'll take you to court. Shame your family."	(Had coffee; not hungry. Went into bedroom)
	1600	Had a bath	(TB looking for something) "Where is it?"	Wife: "What?" TB: "A parcel. Some money You took it."
30-09	1200	TB is fine in the morning		
	1500	Had visitors (their daughers and her husband)	"See the light where it is. Something is wrong with the wire in the ceiling. What is up in the air?"	(Everything was OK)
	1700	Family left	"Come and see the light. We can go to bed comfortable Come on. I'll show you."	(Wife told him everything was all right)
02-10	0830	Had breakfast	"Do we go to school today?"	Wife: "You mean the Day Centre" (at EBHC). TB: "Yes. Are there any kids here to go to school?" (TB was tired and went back to bed)
	1200	Lunch	"There is some outfit coming here today."	Wife: "Who?" TB: "I don't know. Are you going to help me?" (TB puts shoe laces in his shoes) Wife: "With what?" TB: "You don't know yourself." (Went to lie down).

adequately recall and report problematic behaviour and its antecedents. However, she did not often report the consequences of this behaviour in sufficient enough detail to allow for precise analysis. Nevertheless, it was readily apparent that many of the behaviours previously described as "confused" occurred immediately upon awakening or immediately prior to it. In still later ABC reports, it was noted that the naps occurred at predictable times, after lunch in the early afternoon.

Prinz and Raskind (1978) have observed that disorientation upon awakening is fairly common in the aged. Although there

Behavioural Assessment Programme: Patient TB

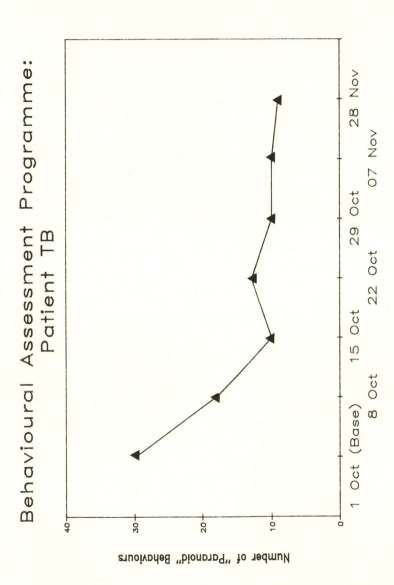

WEEK OF OBSERVATION

FIGURE 1. Week-by-week observations of the number of "paranoid"-type behaviours. The first week (1 Oct) served as a baseline, assessment period. Intervention began in the second week (8 Oct). Note the dramatic decrease in problematic conduct, this tending to stabilize by the third week (15 Oct) remaining at that level for the duration of the observation period.

are only limited data with respect to multiple infarcts, Hachinski et al. (1974) describe nocturnal confusion as being one of the clinical features of this disorder. Excessive daytime sleepiness and resultant confusion may also be common in the elderly (Miles and Dement, 1980). Finally, daytime sleepiness has been found to fluctuate on an approximately 90 minute cycle (Broughton, 1975) and may well peak in the early afternoon during the so-called "post-lunch dip." TB's confusional state therefore appeared to occur during periods of low arousal. The pathological nature of TB's situation was probably due to the deterioration of his temporal lobes with a resultant anterograde amnesia which would surely have added to the "normal" aged degree of confusion following sleep. Finally, although details of consequential actions are only briefly presented, it was apparent that TB's wife was reinforcing the inappropriate behaviour. She often queried his confused statements which consequently led to its continuation as TB attempted to work through his already muddled, "fuzzy" flow of logic.

In the second and subsequent weeks, TB's wife was asked to provide even more detail of her husband's behaviour patterns and to play closer attention to the consequences of her husband's actions. She was told to ignore his confused behaviour (do not respond to his "bizarre," inappropriate questions or if this were not possible, change the topic) as much as possible and to reinforce appropriate behaviours. She was also encouraged to reduce the number of daily naps. The number of confused and paranoid behaviours dropped to 20 in the second week. As is apparent from the samples of the ABC provided in Table 2, these behaviours were still occasionally being reinforced. At the end of the second week of monitoring, instructions were again provided as to the need for reinforcement of proper and the ignoring of inappropriate behaviour. In the weeks that followed, inappropriate behaviour tended to level off to approximately 10 per week. These occurred mainly upon awakening in the morning. In these cases, TB was still unable to sort reality from unreality. The family reported that the reduction of daily naps almost eliminated periods of "nocturnal confusion" (confused, disoriented behaviour following awakenings during the night).

TABLE 2: INTERVENTION PERIOD—2 WEEKS

DATE	TIME	ANTECEDENT BEHAVIOUR	PROBLEM BEHAVIOUR	CONSEQUENTIAL BEHAVIOUR
04-10	1100	Came in the house after gathering leaves and garbage	"Do you need a match to light the stove. (It is electric...No reply to question)	We had lunch. TB then had a nap
	1530	After sleeping	"What day is today?" "Do we go to EBHC tomorrow?"	TB walked around in bedroom and helped to vacuum.
	1900	After dinner	"Are we supposed to got to EBHC tomorrow?" (Looking for something). "Come look at razor. I can't turn it off. It might start a fire. What will I do?"	(Wife continues to watch TV) Wife: "It's OK." (TB continues to look at razor. Wife goes to bed at 2230. TB sits for an hour and says he is afraid. He can't sleep. Went to bed at 2400. Slept with his clothes on.)
05-10	0900	After sleeping	"When do we go to day centre?" (Looks at his appointment reminder. There are 3 copies. Wants wife to write it again.	Wife: "I already have." TB: "It will be fresher."
	1100	Comes down from bedroom after sleeping	Worried about razor. No light on it. "We need an electrician."	
	1115	Daughter called to invite TB and wife to Thanksgiving dinner.	Talked to her abour razor. No light on it.	Daugher replies there never was a light on it.
	1130	Wife going out to bowling	Holds her arm; tore belt off coat. (Wife said she had to go out)	TB talks to neighbour about razor. Asks her about razor. Says he is afraid to stay alone.
	1500	Wife returns from bowling	TB apologizes. won't do it again.	TB walks around.
	1715	Had dinner	"Meal was very good." (TB dries dishes) "Are you sure razor is OK?" Is there any danger of fire?"	Wife: "Leave it on the dresser. It will be easy to find and you won't lose it." TB: "No, no. Somebody will take it."
	2030	Wife locked back door Did not lock front door	"Give me the key"	Wife: "You do not need it." (TB insists he does and continues to do so until he falls asleep at 2230).
06-10	0900	At breakfast	"Where is Katie" (his sister in Ireland) "Are the stores open?" (He means the bank) "I have to get some money." "It is all gone."	Lies down for a 1 hour nap
	1200	At lunch	"Are we alone?" "Somebody took my money. My grandmother is dead. I'll soon be with her."	
07-10	0900	At breakfast	"I wonder who was in the house last night. My money is gone."	Wife: "It was just a dream." (TB walked around and took a nap.)
08-10	0930	At breakfast	"What day is it?" (Wanted to borrow money)	Wife: "You don't need any today." (TB counts his quarters)
	1500		TB putting laces in his shoes	
	1900	TB walking around	Asks where he should hide his roll of money and his quarters.	

DISCUSSION

Behavioural assessment involves the identity of the patient's problem responses in terms of their nature, frequency, intensity, duration and location, before, during and subsequent quent to intervention (Hussian and Davis, 1985). TB had been observed to display paranoid-type behaviour over at least a 3-4 year period prior to this referral to EBHC. Indeed, so severe was the condition that he was eventually admitted to a psychiatric ward where he received drug intervention for his condition. Neurological examination pointed to large infarcts of the temporal lobes. Neuropsychological assessment indicated that TB had a severe anterograde amnesia. While his confusional-disoriented state was likely a result of his memory disorder, it was only after a precise behavioural assessment of his daily home situation that a consistent, antecedent triggering agent became apparent. TB's "paranoid" state most often preceded or followed periods of sleep or naps. A retrospective review of the neuropsychological report (made prior to the behavioural assessment) insightfully predicted, "Excess demands and stimulation will provoke anxiety and confusion. . . . His cognitive deficits may be managed by a treatment program that offers a maximum amount of structure, predictability and consistency." Unknown at the time was the fact that "excess demands and stimulation" provoked fatigue which appears to be the triggering agent for subsequent confusion. TB's wife, by caringly responding to her husband's confused, disoriented questions, unwittingly lead to their continuation by evoking further confusion, anxiety and in all likelihood, subsequent fatigue and exasperation. As she learned to withold responding to these behaviours, they manifested a dramatic decline. The paranoid-type behaviours have not reached a stable level and occur at quite predictable times. It is possible, but we feel unlikely, that specific polygraphic monitoring of his sleep patterns may provide a means for altering his sleep patterns, perhaps alleviating the problem altogether.

REFERENCES

Broughton, R. (1975). Biorhythmic variations in consciousness and psychological functions. *Canadian Psychological Review, 16,* 217–239.

Hachinski, V.C., Lassen, N.A., and Marshall, J. (1974). Multi-infarct dementia. A cause of mental deterioration in the elderly. *Lancet, 2,* 207–210.

Hussian, R.A. and Davis, R.L. (1985). *Responsive care: Behavioral Intervention with elderly persons.* Champaign, Illinois: Research Press.

Miles, L. and Dement, W. (1980). Sleep and aging. *Sleep, 3,* 119–220.

Prinz, P. and Raskind, M. (1978). Aging and sleep disorders. In R. Williams and I. Karacan (Eds.), *Sleep Disorders: Diagnosis and Treatment.* (New York: Wiley, 303–321.)

Chapter 15:
Music Therapy and Staff Stress

Bright begins by echoing the perspectives of Burr and Weiner/White: uncooperativeness is a label which the staff puts on patients who are difficult to manage. Therefore, uncooperativeness is really somebody else's problem: the problem of the person with whom the patient will not cooperate. In an institutional setting, uncooperativeness in patients means stress for staff.

Bright therefore begins by measuring the level and kind of stress experienced by staff, and then moves to the question of how the staff uses music in an attempt to deal with such stress. This is supplemented with some excellent and specific suggestions for using music with institutionalized patients.

The use of music in therapy with the aged has been discussed in previous issues of *CG:*

I (2) 76–77
III (2) 40–41

as has the use of art, movement, and poetry:

II (1) 45–63
II (2) 67
III (3) 46–47, 89–90

The Use of Music Therapy and Activities With Demented Patients Who Are Deemed "Difficult to Manage"

Ruth Bright, BMus, CMT

INTRODUCTION

Over some 25 years, nurses have commented to the present author that even demented patients respond to music, and that their behaviour is not only "better" (more tolerable to staff?) during the music session but that there appears often to be some degree of carry-over into general ward behaviour for a time afterwards.

In order to investigate this, it was dediced to find out which behaviours are most difficult for nursing staff to cope with, and then to see how music therapy may be used most effectively. Styles of intervention are discussed, to see which are the most helpful in achieving personal satisfaction for the patients, and also for improving everyday ward atmosphere for staff and patients through the music-based relationships.

This paper is the outcome of that investigation.

MANAGEABLE OR UNMANAGEABLE?

In general, those who work with demented patients tend to concentrate on their positive attributes and their pleasanter personality traits rather than on the problems. However, in view of the incidence of staff burn-out, it is also important that we do consider from time to time the difficulties which

Ms. Bright is Music Therapist, Rozelle Hospital and War Memorial Hospital, Sydney, New South Wales, Australia.

131

are experienced, even if only in order to devise ways of minimizing them.

The concepts of manageable, unmanageable or difficult-to-manage are, in practical terms, relative matters only. For example, a person with only a moderate impairment may be considered to be unmanageable at home if she lives alone and has a degree of memory loss such that she is likely to leave a pan of hot fat on the stove and set fire to the house, forget that she has taken medication such as a digitalis preparation and take a second dose (resulting in toxicity), or if there is a degree of paranoia such that the door is barred against Meals on Wheels (and nutrition is is compromised). On the other hand, someone with these problems would present only minimal difficulty if he or she were living under appropriate supervision in a frail aged hostel. Extremely difficult behaviour is seen in the incontinent man with violent aggression towards anyone who approaches him, who would be regarded as unmanageable by relatives at home, or in a nursing home where there is a low staffing ratio, but would be regarded only as "difficult to manage" in a hospital with adequate staffing levels, where two people can distract or restrain him from violence whilst a third person changes his wet pyjamas.

The person being cared for at home may cause so much distress to the family that he or she is regarded as "impossible to keep at home" (i.e., unmanageable) if the behaviour is emotionally intolerable. Greene and colleagues (Green, 1981) described the behaviour which carers in the home find stressful, and noted that what is commonly perceived as stressful is the change in the relative from an active, involved person to a withdrawn and isolated person, with marked changes of mood, and yet a nurse, who is emotionally uninvolved, may not be so distressed by the changes. Perhaps there is a parallel here with responses noted in relatives of head injury patients (Proctor, 1973). Bodily change is relatively easy to accept, and what is most difficult to adapt to is the change in personality.

We can, however, look at manageability in terms of staff stress within institutions, and it is this aspect which was considered in the preparation of this paper.

"Stress" is used throughout this article in the everyday common usage of the word, rather than in Selye's concept of useful stress which helps us to develop and mature (Selye, 1975).

When we consider the stress experienced by staff in caring

for those with advanced dementia, we may think of stressful sensory stimuli that are experienced. We are affected by sound, e.g., from patients who shout frequently, or constantly grumble and complain, from constant verbal abuse, from constant crying. We are affected also through our sense of smell—from incontinence of faeces and urine, and the other body ordours that cannot always be removed. We are affected through the sense of touch when we have to clear up stained clothes and bed linen, and through sight, e.g., when we have to see table manners that revolt us, clothes stained with food, disinhibited sexual behaviour, trails of faeces along the floor where an incontinent patient has walked, and so on. These all overlap with psychosocial stress, as also do situations where we observe and try to prevent verbal and physical abuse by a violent patient towards fellow-residents, when we try to persuade patients to take life-preserving medication or drink adequate fluids, try to keep within the ward a person who is constantly trying to escape to "get home to feed the baby," etc.

We may also suffer from loss of self-esteem, in itself a stressful experience, because of our inability keep things running smoothly, and from the accusations—however groundless—which may be levelled at us by angry or paranoid patients.

The extent to which we are able to cope may be altered by our attitudes and also by our social support systems, although this is somewhat a matter for conjecture. There is also a suggestion that Type A personalities are more at risk of stress than are Type B people. (Tennant,1985).

If the perfectionist is indeed more at risk of stress than the easy-going person, this may well explain some of the stress of work with the demented, where cleanliness, planning, neatness and timetables are impossible to achieve without undue pressure being placed upon both patients and staff, and where the unforeseeable is the rule!

FINDING OUT ABOUT STAFF STRESS

No attempt was made to measure harmful stress physiologically. It was decided that the perceptions of the staff about their own degree of stress were more important in this particular context than any attempt to prove or disprove the correctness of these perceptions.

A questionnaire was drawn up after consultation with nurses at a variety of levels, who were asked what kind of behaviour caused them to feel that they were suffering from stress. The behaviours suggested were then collated, and overlapping suggestions were combined as accurately as possible, in order to prevent the questionnaire being impossibly long. Two sections (B & D of the questionnaire), concerned with personal ways of coping with stress, produced such diverse results, without any immediately obvious statistical significance of association, that they have been omitted from this paper, but will be analysed by other methods for possible later publication.

In drawing up the questionnaire, it was hypothesised that the level of nursing or other education might be one factor affecting stress, in that coping with difficult behaviour could perhaps be easier for the highly educated person who understands the reasons for the behaviours. Respondents were therefore asked to give their professional status. Preliminary consideration of the data does not support the hypothesis.

On the other hand, the extent to which one is held responsible for patients' well-being might be more of a source of stress to registered staff compared with unregistered, since it is the Registered Nurses who normally carry the ultimate responsibility. Again, preliminary consideration of data did not support this hypothesis. Some of the highest and some of the lowest individual stress totals were reported both by Directors of Nursing, and by Nursing Aides who have little or no formal training and no heavy burden of legal liability. [Statistical comparisons of these aspects of perceived stress in in registered and unregistered staff will, it is hoped, be the topic for a later publication.]

Morale of a unit was also seen as a possible modifying factor, in that an individual working in a unit which lacks good team morale may experience more stress than a person who works with supportive colleagues. There does appear to be a difference in reported stress from one unit to another, but whether this is due to team morale or some other factor is not yet certain.

Respondents were asked to fill in replies to a section concerned with the actual music activities in their unit. It was known that none of the units has a full music *Therapy* programme, but that—depending on individual talents, time and interests—some music activities probably took place, even if this was only a matter of selection of an appropriate radio station.

The questionnaire was administered informally to staff working in two types of establishments in which persons suffering from advanced dementia are cared for. Four of the units were wards in a large State-run institution, three were Church-run nursing homes where there are substantial numbers of dementia sufferers, and one unit was a privately-run nursing home with special interests in, and programmes for, dementia sufferers.

Post-graduate students in two Gerontological Nursing courses also filled out the questionnaire, all of these subjects being Registered Nurses. Most patients being cared for by respondents to the questionnaire suffered from Alzheimer's disease, but there were also some with:

—Multi-infarct dementia.
—Dementia following a single stroke.
—Parkinsonian dementia.
—Huntington's disease.
—Late-onset schizophrenia and other psychiatric illnesses.
—Psychotic depression with organic features.
—Extreme neurotic depression.
—Brain damage resulting from head injuries.
—Alcohol-related brain damage with dementia.
—Dementia of advanced Down's syndrome.
—A combination of two or more of these.

THE QUESTIONNAIRE

MUSIC THERAPY AND THE DIFFICULT-TO-MANAGE DEMENTED PATIENT

Part A

There are various behaviours which lead staff to see patients as "difficult," and one way of estimating the degree of difficulty in management seems to be to measure the perception of stress caused by their behaviours. Printed below is a list of behaviours, and you are asked to rate them for the amount of stress YOU PERSONALLY experience according to the following 5-point rating scale:

0 = causes me no stress.
1 = causes me a little stress
2 = causes me moderate stress
3 = causes me considerable stress.
4 = causes me intolerable stress.

Behaviour   *Rating*

  1. Verbally aggressive behaviour to staff.   —
  2. Physically aggressive behaviour to staff.   —
  3. Verbally aggressive behaviour to fellow-patients.   —
  4. Physically aggressive behaviour to fellow-patients.   —
  5. Shouting, generally noisy behaviour.   —
  6. Grumbling, complaining, accusations.   —
  7. Incontinence of urine.   —
  8. Incontinence of faeces.   —
  9. Overt sexual behaviour, masturbation in public.   —
 10. Refusing to eat meals.   —
 11. Refusing to drink.   —
 12. Refusing to take medication.   —
 13. Refusing to co-operate in ward programme.   —
 14. Constant efforts to leave ward/unit.   —
 15. Repeated confused questionning.   —
 16. Interfering with other people's property.   —
 17. Greedy behaviour, trying to steal food.   —
 18. Messy eating, food on clothes.   —
 19. Day/night reversal.   —
 20. Constant crying and sadness.   —

Part B is omitted here, for reasons stated above.

Part C

I use music to help me cope with patients in various ways:

1. Singing with patients as I get them dressed. . . .
2. Singing with patients as we walk along . . .
3. Choosing a radio station that plays the kind of music the patients like. . . .
4. Putting on tapes or records of the kind of music that is familiar to them. . . .
5. Talking to them individually about memories connected with music. . . .
6. Talking to the patients in a group about memories connected with music. . . .
7. Using music to enhance exercise programmes. . . .
8. Helping to organise singalongs etc.. . . .
9. Using percussion instruments for music sessions. . . .
10. Using music to enhance other programmes, e.g., Reality Orientation, . . . Quiz, . . . Newspaper session
11. Using music to distract those who are angry/upset etc. . . .
12. Other . . .

Part D omitted here, to be discussed below.

WHAT WAS FOUND OUT

Behaviour/Stress Tables

A hundred and eleven questionnaires were completed; of the subjects, 59 were Registered Nurses, 45 were unregistered nurses, and seven subjects were involved in non-nursing duties such as podiatry and recreation, but were in close contact with patients.

Stress rating was measured by totalling the stress ratings recorded for the 20 behaviours listed. The possible range was from 0–80, actual range 1–50. Mean for the entire population was 24.88, Standard deviation was 12.63, Ratio of mean to standard deviation was 1.97. Hence, the degree of confidence that the behaviours listed are, on the whole, stressful exceeds 95%. (We are looking at only one "tail" of the frequency distribution.)

Individual Behaviours

(Please refer back to the list in Part A.)

Behaviour	Mean	Stand. Dev.	Ratio
4	2.468	1.016	2.43
2	1.937	1.064	1.82
20	1.667	0.994	1.68
14	1.604	1.114	1.68
3	1.559	0.997	1.56
5	1.432	1.076	1.33
16	1.297	0.940	1.38

Above this line, it is reasonable to assume that the behaviours are generally productive of stress in hospital/nursing home nursing staff, in that they are significantly different from zero at the 90% confidence level.

9	1.288	1.238	1.04
1	1.270	1.044	1.22
6	1.207	1.019	1.18
11	1.099	1.026	1.07
15	1.072	1.024	1.05
12	1.063	1.021	1.04
19	0.963	1.017	0.95
10	0.882	0.922	0.96
8	0.774	0.891	0.87
18	0.676	0.906	0.75
13	0.613	0.777	0.79
7	0.405	0.652	0.62

From the spread of scores we may conclude that perceived stress varies from one person to another, and that there must be factors influencing this. No conclusion can at present be drawn as to what these factors are.

The behaviours in which respondents perceived themselves as having lower stress varied as to category, but No. 9 (overt sexual behaviour, masturbation in public) is interesting in that the figures reflect what had been expected—that this is a highly individual matter. It is a behaviour which distresses some staff greatly, but leaves others entirely unperturbed.

The one behaviour which was given a positive stress rating

was No. 4, physical aggression to fellow-patients. The figures are significant well above the 95% confidence level. Presumably, the carer is stressed by the unpredictability of the behaviour, and the feeling of personal helplessness, together with empathy for the helplessness of the patient who is attacked. Incontinence of either urine or faeces was rated low, and one may speculate that this is because it is something which is readily dealt with by nursing staff.

Staff Music Activities

The frequency of each music activity carried out by nurses are listed below:

Activity	*Frequency*
3. Choosing the radio station to suit patients' preference.	98
4. Putting on recordings to suit patients' preferences.	89
5. Talking individually about associations with music.	64
2. Singing with patients as you walk along.	59
1. Singing as patients are dressed in the morning.	57
11. Using music to distract those who are angry, upset.	57
6. Talking with groups about associations with music.	51
7. Using music to enhance exercises.	50
8. Singalongs.	49
10. Using music in quizzes, reality orientation, etc.	23
9. Percussion instrument work.	22
12. Other.	9

No. 12, "Other," included religious music for services, music for dancing, concerts by staff or visitors.

Part D of the questionnaire was concerned with attitudes to music, whether or not it helped nursing staff to feel closer to difficult patients, helped them to cope in the ward. The type of music was unspecified, and in fact it appeared likely that in many instances it consisted mainly of radio and recorded music (see rating of 3 & 4 above). Results were not significant, and this is probably because:

a. there is no regular programme in music therapy in any of the included;
b. the establishments vary greatly in the extent to which music is used, depending on interests and skills of nursing staff;
c. insufficient information was given in the questionnaire as to what, e.g., "Music in the ward" actually implied.

Nevertheless, the individual answers (some of which included personal comments) indicated a general enthusiasm for having more music available, together with recognition of the difficulties for nurses who have no special skills in music. An exception was a nurse who wrote that she disliked having music in the ward because it built up an association in her mind between music and work-related stress, and that this carried over into her private life, thereby spoiling her personal enjoyment of music.

Because of the relatively small number of nurses who reported practical skills in playing a musical instrument—a total of only 27, of whom several noted "*very* badly!" it is clear that the responses to Nos. 3 & 4 of this section represent the general state of musical activities, i.e., mainly recordings and radio music. One assumes that the employment of a professional music therapist as a visiting specialist or a permanent staff member would change this situation markedly.

HOW CAN MUSIC THERAPY REDUCE STAFF STRESS?

It is interesting to consider how many of the stress-producing behaviours listed in Section A would be reduced or even temporarily eliminated by a full program of music therapy. Music therapists are trained to work in dementia, and their training covers not only knowledge and understanding of the organic basis for dementia and difficult behaviour generally, but also the psychosocial aspects of emotional and psychiatric illness in the elderly. These include the prevalence of unresolved griefs and anger in the aged, including persons with advanced dementia. They also learn appropriate techniques for displacing anger and restlessness through appropriate music techniques, and so on. The use of music in counselling, for the amelioration of depressive and other illness, has long been advocated by the present author (Bright, 1972, 1981, 1982, 1985, 1986).

For full effectiveness there must be provision for group and individual work in music therapy. The group "singalong" or percussion band session does have merit, but if this is all we do, we fail to meet the needs of the withdrawn and isolated, the sad and the depressed (the two are by no means synonymous), nor the very special needs of those with aphasia in varying degrees of impairment, those with impairment of body image and perceptual problems in general, the individual needs of the dying, the visually and/or hearing-impaired clients, the person with neurological disease or impairment (such as "stroke"), the older developmentally-delayed client, and so on. All of these problems may be met in those who also have organic brain dysfunction, and, even without such damage, those with the difficulties listed above can be "difficult," if their psychosocial needs are not met.

It is an unfortunate fact that many programmes of music ACTIVITY carried out with no therapeutic aims or objectives, no assessment or evaluation, are labelled as Music THERAPY when it is in fact RECREATION.

That there is value in recreation is undeniable, but if we provide ONLY this for our demented and difficult patients, we are failing to give them the best available help. We must be willing to work within a framework of understanding the cognitive, social, physical and emotional deficits in dementia. We must have extensive practical music skills, not merely be able to operate a tape player or play a few standard tunes or songs, and hand out tambourines and triangles. We must also be able and willing to use the same skills of assessment, evaluation and planning which we would expect to use in, e.g., stroke rehabilitation or child psychiatry.

When planning music therapy, the size of the group is critical, and as a general rule one can work on the principle that the more deteriorated the patients, the smaller the group must be. With highly disturbed persons, a one-to-one interaction may be essential in order to establish a relationship, although one would hope ultimately to achieve some measure of group interaction.

The presence of helpers is also important, since, when working with a group of demented persons, one person cannot alone carry out all that is needed. One must have someone available to toilet patients if necessary, assist in stimulating participants in mobility work such as clapping or foot-tapping if this is included, join in the singing, dancing or playing of musical instruments, and helping the participants to select the instrument of their choice from those which are offered to them. "Choice" and "offered" are the crucial words—we must never force instruments upon people as if they were children.

Music skills of the therapist must include the playing of a *portable* instrument, it is critical that one maintains eye contact with each participant in turn by moving around the group, the piano is almost useless for work in dementia. The guitar is popular in the USA but it is not really the instrument of choice in work with the elderly, many of whom have such hearing loss that all they hear is the voice of the therapist singing without any of the harmonic support of the accompanying instrument. In Australia the piano accordion is regarded as almost essential for work in geriatrics because it is more familiar than the guitar, and because it gives a strong harmonic structure to the music. In addition, the bass can be played with one hand whilst the therapist sings the melody, leaving the therapist with a free hand for physical contact with the patient.

The ability to transpose is also critical. This is, one assumes, a skill which is universal for practising professional music therapists, but may not be so for other people who can be involved in music programmes for the aged. Many books of songs are written in keys which only concert artists can sing comfortably, and, if the participation of group members is to be gained, we must play the music at a pitch in which it can easily be sung. The speed at which music is played is also important. It must be appropriate to the current status of the participants, and not galloping away ahead!

When an emotional component to the dementia is suspected, the therapist must have in-depth knowledge and skills in counseling so that music may be used to elicit the underlying problem such as guilt and unresolved grief. But this is not appropriate for group work in the ward; the intervention must take place in complete privacy and confidentiality.

In an article of this length, no details can be given of how to carry out music therapy programmes but a summary appears below of the main areas in which changes to behaviour have been noticed as a consequence of music therapy programmes.

Wandering. Patients tend to "stay put" during music group.

Aggression. Having a pleasant activity which engages the attention reduces the likelihood of aggression, both physically and verbally.

Agitation. This is observed as part of *depression,* but may result from memory loss (as when a woman tries to get home to her long-dead husband, fearing that he will be home looking for her), but may also result from unfinished business such as guilt over divorce long past, difficulty in believing that a middle-aged child really is dead, and so on. Individual work in which music is used specifically to elicit hidden or repressed material can effect changes even in people who have an organic dementia, since reactive depression from an unresolved grief or guilt exacerbates organic dementia, and may actually be the cause of a pseudo-dementia (McAllister, 1983). Music therapy with counselling has in many instances proven highly effective in depression and in resolving agitation by providing symbolic forgiveness, restitution etc. (Bright, 1986).

Apathy. Well-chosen music, appropriate to the current cognitive and memory status of the client, helps to enliven both individuals and groups. For some, it is essential to use music from very old memory traces, but, for a person who is more cognitively intact, music of a more recent era is useful.

Physical *inertia* may also be overcome by judicious use of music to enhance mobility work.

Unsuspected springs of *creativity* may be brought to light by instrumental work on tuned and untuned percussion instruments, through improvisation and, to a lesser extent, by the so-called Rhythm Band. The disadvantage of the latter is that all too easily it becomes a mindless thumping on instruments handed out at random, which may give a sense of achievement to the organiser but is likely to inflict institutionalisation, or boredom or humiliation upon the hapless participants!

It is important to note that there may be generalisation to

everyday behaviour, as Odell has noted in Cambridge, U.K., where previously antagonistic patients worked together in music session, and continued their good relationship within the ward for a substantial period of time (Odell, 1986).

But, even where there is not a sustained generalisation, staff attitudes towards patients hitherto deemed to be difficult or unmanageable may be altered, so that the patient who has participated in music therapy is afterwards perceived as "more interesting than I thought," "still a real person" and so on.

This is in itself important for both staff and patient morale. We cannot ignore these possibilities for using music therapy with the "difficult-to-manage" patient. It is clearly not enough to leave it to the individual motivation and chance music skills of nurses on the job. We must provide a profess-sional music therapy service for the aged, as the community expects to be provided for the (more appealing?) *child* who is autistic, physically disabled, disabled, intellectually disadvantaged. By providing a service we improve not only the quality of life for the clients, (and—if they are able to attend—assisting the emotional needs of relatives) but we also reduce stress levels and burn-out problems of the nursing staff; even if this is only a temporary benefit, it is worth having!

REFERENCES

Greene, J.G. et al. (1982). Measuring Behavioural Disturbance of Elderly Demented Patients in the Community and its effects of Relatives. A Factor Analytic Study. Age & Ageing; *11*, 121–126.

Proctor, H. (1973). Head Injuries. Physiotherapy, *59, (12)*, 10, December, 380–382.

Selye, H. (1975). Stress without Distress. Hodder & Stoughton, U.K., p. 31.

Tennant, C. et al. (1985). The Concept of Stress. Australia and New Zealand Journal of Psychiatry, *19(2)*, June, 113–119.

Bright, R. (1972). Music in Geriatric Care, Angus & Robertson, Australia (US Edition Musicgraphics, 1980), p. 73.

Bright, R. (1981, i). Practical Planning in Music Therapy for the Aged. Musicgraphics, USA, p. 33 onwards.

Bright, R. (1981, ii). Music and the Management of Grief Reactions. In Burnside (Ed.), Nursing and the Aged, Mcgraw-Hill, USA, p. 141 onwards.

McAllister, T.W. (1983). Pseudodementia: an Overview. American Journal of Psychiatry, *140*, 5, pp. 528–533.

Bright, R. (in preparation, 1986). Grieving. M.M.B. St. Louis, USA.

Odell, H. (1985). Cambridge, U.K., Personal Communication re research project (unpublished).

Chapter 16:
Music and Exercise: A Great Combination

Meddaugh continues Bright's emphasis on the importance of viewing patient uncooperativeness as the staff's problem. Following through on the topic of abuse of staff by the patients in her previous chapter (6), Meddaugh now offers a solution: exercise to music. The small sample size of this pilot project and the tentative nature of some of the outcome measures precludes this from being definitive, but Meddaugh's listing of specific procedures makes this a valuable how-to for staffs wishing to cope with abusive patients.

A topic related to physical exercise, that of yoga, has been covered in a previous issue of *CG:*

III (4) 45–51

Exercise-to-Music
for the Abusive Patient

Dorothy I. Meddaugh, MS, RN

This essay will address a mental health problem, staff abuse by the elderly institutionalized skilled nursing home patient, and one intervention which was used in an attempt to improve behavior of a group of assaultive patients. The plan for the intervention, as well as the positive and negative outcomes ensuing from the intervention will be described.

STATEMENT OF THE PROBLEM

The addressed problem of staff abuse within a skilled nursing unit in a large county-run long term care facility had been noted by the nursing staff for two years. The incident reports and chart nursing notes indicated the time and type of abuse toward care providers. Anecdotal information indicated that the staff abuse problem had decreased morale on the unit and had increased the anxiety level of the care provider.

Optimal care can most likely occur in any atmosphere where there is a minimum of stress, to the care provider as well as to the patient. When abuse of the staff by the patient occurs, the patient may feel anxious because of loss of control and staff may be hesitant and frightened about caring for the patient. This stressful situation may result in less than optimal care for these abusive residents.

As a graduate student in the field of gerontological nursing, this writer was approached by the nurse manager of the Skilled Nursing Facility (SNF) floor on which nine abusive patients resided. The nurse manager desired an intervention for these nine people hopefully resulting in fewer unacceptable acting-out behaviors such as spitting, hitting, or scratching. Neither inclusion in activity groups nor one-to-one interventions had

147

proven successful in lessening these unacceptable behaviors. There were no other apparent resources available in the institution to meet the psychosocial needs of the abusive patients.

Assessment of the nine patients who regularly physically abused the staff was completed within a two week time period. Four abusers, 45% of the nine, were female. Five abusers, 56% of the nine, were male. Most of the abuser group were dependent in activities of daily living and most were termed "confused" by the nursing staff. The average age of the abusive patient was 75 years. All of the abusive patients were considered by the nursing staff to exhibit regressive behavior. Observationally, it was noted that, except for "bed and body" routine care and feeding times, there was very little verbal communication between staff members and the abusive patients. Usually, the abusive patients remained in their rooms all day. It was hard to discern whether this was by personal choice or by the choice of the nursing staff. It was decided that whatever intervention was instituted should incorporate within its framework the following goals: (1) to alert the abusive residents to their surroundings and to present events, (2) to provide opportunities for verbal and social interpersonal exchange, (3) to offer an acceptable way for channeling feelings of anxiety, frustration and hopelessness and (4) to assist each abusive person in regaining a sense of self-worth and personal dignity.

INTERVENTION

Literature was reviewed regarding the role of exercise in the life of the elderly person. Since all nine abusive patients seemed to get very little exercise, it was felt that physical activity could be one of the main components of the program to be instituted.

Luther and Price (1980) stated that people who exercise regularly "improve their efficiency in performing submaximal physical activities, feel better, improve their self-image, sleep better, and have less anxiety and depression" (Luther & Price p. 517, 1980). They also stated that exercise programs for the elderly person can significantly increase strength and flexibility.

According to Heinzlman and Bagley (1970), exercise can

produce positive effects which include a greater ability to cope with stress and tension as well as a more positive self image. Still other positive results were found when Powell (1974) examined the cognitive ability of institutionalized elderly mental patients. He found that exercise programs raised the cognitive ability of the patients significantly more than did a social interaction program.

Needler and Baer (1982) offered the techniques of music, movement and remotivation as they are used with regressed elderly patients in a long-term care institution. Their results indicated that this program maintained or reestablished physical and mental alertness, expanded capabilities, stimulated social interactions and reintroduced an awareness to the outside world. Residents laughed, relaxed, communicated feelings and developed friendships when they were together in the group. Hoskyns (1982) found these same findings when working with a group of patients with Huntington's Chorea.

A question that could be asked is whether or not a person who has found unacceptable ways of releasing feelings of frustration and aggression could learn to release such feelings in acceptable ways. Oberleder (1976) states that almost all behavior can improve when the care provider is willing to be patient. He states that one must wait until some remnant of desired behavior shows itself. This behavior must then be rewarded promptly with a smile, a pat, or even a hug. Behavior that is consistently rewarded will be repeated, and behavior that is ignored will become extinct. The care provider can work only with behaviors already present. Therefore, the agitated patient can be rewarded for sitting still or for a natural pause in his screaming.

The literature review indicated that a viable option for an intervention for abusive patients would incorporate both music and exercise. It was, therefore, decided that the program should be an exercise-to-music group which would incorporate within its framework the principles of positive reinforcement of desired behavior.

An outcome measurement tool was devised in order to keep records on each member of the group of abusers. Information kept on a chart included a description of the social interaction of each resident, of the willingness to try to do the exercises, of the ability to do the exercises, of any acceptable behavior, of any unacceptable behavior and of any extinction of unacceptable behavior. Small improvements in any of these areas would indicate a positive outcome. The group met three times a week for nine weeks. A set plan for each group meeting was devised to incorporate the idea gained from Needler & Baer (1982) that structure and repetition is needed in working with the regressed elderly patient (see Table 1).

Table 1

Exercise-to-music group

1. play music softly - Chase the Clouds, Soft

2. notice weather

3. thank all for coming

4. point out who is missing from group and reason why

5. go to each group member, touch their hand, address them by

   name and welcome them

6. exercises - set pattern (see Table 2)

   a. help those who cannot follow directions - patterning

   b. enlist help of those who can do exercises

   c. reinforce all attempts to do exercises

7. accept all behaviors, at first

   a. ignore negative

   b. praise positive

   after time - talk quietly with each member who does

   unacceptable behavior about it and reinforce attempts to

   extinguish such behavior

8. play game - balls into bucket

   a. praise all attempts

   b. use voice at bucket level to guide three blind patients

   c. clap for bull's eye

9. end of session - go to each member, touch hand, call by name,

   thank each for coming, reinforce individual efforts

10. announce to the group when we'll be together again

RESULTS OF THE INTERVENTION

Before the study period, the staff were asked how well the abusive group of patients would follow directions. They indicated that the group would not be able to follow directions and hence would not participate in the exercises planned for the group. The staff felt it would be a major accomplishment if the abusive patients would at least consent to attend the exercise-to-music group sessions.

At the beginning of the study period, attempts to accomplish the exercises were sporadic and the patients were not able to do many of the exercises very well. At the end of the nine week period the members of the abusive group were evaluated. All of the abusive patients except one participated at least once weekly. The abusive patient participated an average of 1.5 times per week. Positive results included an increase in overall ability to do the exercises (see Table 2 for exercises used with this group) due to the repetition of doing the same exercises over time.

Three of the more alert group members were able to do all of the exercises while only one of the group members did not do any of the exercises. It was not apparent if the one group member who did not do the exercises was physically unable, refused to do the exercises or simply could not follow directions. The ability of the three more alert group members to perform the exercises helped to encourage increased participation by the remainder of the group. A frequency table of the ability of the patient to perform a specific exercise appears in Table 3.

Any success seemed to foster feelings of positive self-concept. One of the patients decreased his verbal swearing at other group members. A few of the group members talked to one another or smiled at each other from time to time.

Staff morale seemed to improve as staff observed group members smile, attempt a new exercise or say "thank you." On the other hand, some abusers chose not to consistently attend some of the special activity sessions. Not all unacceptable behaviors were extinguished within the activity sessions.

The SNF unit decided to continue the intervention after the

services of the graduate student were no longer available. Therefore, two nurses aides were taught how to lead the group. After these aides had led the group for a time, the plan was to teach other aides how to lead the group, thereby ensuring continuity of the intervention.

Table 2

Exercises

1. head back (1) head forward (2)

   five each direction

2. ear toward the shoulder

   1) to the right and then head upright

   2) to the left and then head upright

   five each direction

3. shoulder shrugs

   1) up

   2) down

   five each direction

4. rotation of shoulders

   1) frontward

   2) backward

   five each direction

5. arm circles - arms out, palms down

   1) ten forward

   2) ten backward

6. finger flexion and extension

   ten each of clenching and extending

7. finger spreading - arms straight out, palms facing down,

   spread fingers wide apart and then bring them together - ten

8. legs extended - leg out straight for five seconds, one at a

   time - five each

9. rotating ankles - extend each leg and rotate ankle for five

   seconds - five each   (Frankel & Richard, 1980)

Table 3

Exercise ability by nine abusive patients.

Exercise	ability n=9	percent
head front	6	67
head back	4	44
ear to shoulder	8	89
shoulder shrugs	3	33
shoulder rotation	3	33
arm circles	4	44
finger flexion	3	33
finger extension	3	33
finger spreading	6	67
legs extended	7	78
rotating ankles	6	67

RECOMMENDATION FOR THE FUTURE

This intervention for the abusive patient group was successful. There was in increase in the ability of the group members to follow directions. The smiles of the group members indicated their support of the program. However, the intervention had not been in place for a long enough time period to ascertain whether or not these changes were helpful in other areas of the daily life of the abusive patients. A much longer time period would be needed to ascertain carry-over of positive outcomes of the intervention.

The staff of the nursing care unit were not involved in the planning or implementing of the intervention. They did not whole-heartedly support the intervention until they were involved in the leadership roles. It is for this reason that, in future program implementation, the unit staff will be asked to contribute in leadership roles. It is hoped that this will foster the involvement of staff in the project and facilitate the outside group leader in the role of change agent.

REFERENCES

Frankel, S. & Richard, L. (1980) *Be alive as long as you live.* New York: Lippincott & Cromwell.
Heinzelman, F. & Bagley, R.W. (1970) Response to physical activity programs and their effects on health behavior. *Public Health Report, 85,* (10), 905–911.

Hoskyns, S. (1982) The right chord. *Nursing Mirror,* 14–17.
Luther, S.L. & Price, J.H. (1980) Physical fitness: Its role in health for the elderly. *Journal of Gerontological Nursing, 6,* (9), 517–523.
Needler, W. & Baer, M.A. (1982) Movement, music and remotivation with the regressed elderly. *Journal of Gerontological Nursing, 8,* (9), 497–503.
Oberleder, M. (1976) Managing problem behaviors of elderly patients. *Hospital & Community Psychiatry, 27,* (5), 325-9.
Powell, R.R. (1974) Psychological effects of exercise therapy upon institutionalized geriatric mental patients. *Journal of Gerontology, 29,* (2), 157–161.

Chapter 17:
The Outpatient Team

Here Kirk describes one program which succeded in overcoming uncooperative patients by involving not only the skills of the separate team
members, but community and family resources. The necessity for multidisciplinary teams has been a topic of several articles in *CG,* including a
previous special issue:

II (3) 47–54, 64–74
III (2) 38–40
III (3) 23–34

A Community Mental Health Center's Approach to Handling the Uncooperative Aging Client: "Team Approach"

Greg Kirk, MSW

The team concept approach was developed out of concern for the well-being of older persons who were being referred to the Center. Its purpose was to evaluate and treat older persons utilizing professional staff, support agencies, family members and the client. The team consisted of a Geriatric Specialist, a Physician or Psychiatrist, a Social Worker, family members and the client (if able).

The Center's professional staff was encountering an ever increasing number of older clients who were very uncooperative in therapy. Reasons for the hostile behavior ranged from the fear of a mental health center and being sent to an institution to hypochondriasis. The professional staff was getting to a point where no one wanted to treat anyone over age 60. Therefore, the Center Administration decided to do something and the team concept approach was created.

An older person, upon referral to the Center, will be given an appointment with a team of staff members including a Physician or Psychiatrist, Geriatric Specialist, and a Social Worker. The Center also requests that family members and/or significant others join the conference along with the patient. During this conference, a treatment plan is agreed upon by the client with family and mental health staff present. Also, during this time questions are answered, family education and support is provided and any necessary referrals or linkages with other support services or agencies are secured.

The author is with Waccamaw Center for Mental Health, Conway, SC.

The team approach proved very effective with the uncoop- erative aging client. Reasons for the success of this approach are as follows:

1. The client was able to participate in his or her treatment and thus be more receptive to treatment.
2. The relatives that were involved helped relieve a lot of the client's stress and fears as well as having the oppor- tunity to convince an older client of what was in his or her best interest.
3. Having a Physician on the team helped legitimize the cause of treatment selected.
4. The family's knowledge about their loved one's condi- tion helped increase their participation and support.
5. Completing the assessment, treatment plan, and any linkages with other agencies on the same day contrib- uted to the success of the program.

The limitations of the program involved staff time, but this was overcome after a few months of practice. The normal time period for a team conference is between one and one- half hours to two hours.

We also found that older persons enjoyed a group ap- proach to handling their problems as opposed to a one-on-one situation. The benefits from a team approach in working with older uncooperative persons far outweigh the disadvantages.

Chapter 18:
The Team Approach
for Hypochondriasis

Along with paranoia, hypochondriasis is a delusional illness in which elders may refuse to admit the mental nature of their problems. The authors present the case of a 60 year old female fitting the pattern of geriatric hypochondriasis: multiple somatic complaints complicated by depression. The physician treated the patient's verifiable physical disorders while the psychologist used self-management strategies for the depression. Favorable results included a reduction in the number of office visits as well as the frequency of crying, number of somatic complaints, and difficulty in walking.

Previous issues of *CG* have covered hypochondriasis:

I (1) 97–98
I (2) 45–50
I (3) 94–95
II (1) 63–66
III (1) 64–70

and self management techniques:

I (3) 45–52
IV (1) 72–73
IV (2) 38–40, 48–51

Managing an Uncooperative Patient: A Physician-Psychologist Team Approach

Randy T. Kohl, MD
Rick McNeese, PhD
Michael G. Kaven, MA

Until 1980, little behavioral or therapeutic research was devoted to the study of the elderly. In fact, Wisocki and Mosher (1982) noted that of the journals surveyed, only .6% of the articles published used elderly as subjects. While in recent years this trend appears to be reversing, one area of need that remains is psychotherapy for elderly patients. According to Wisocki and Mosher's (1982) review of behavioral gerontology journals, only 5.6% of the articles published dealt with issues of psychotherapy. Thus, the therapist must search for therapeutic ways to deal with an ever-increasing number of unique problems that are presented by the elderly patient.

Not only is there less information available on psychotherapeutic efforts with the elderly, but this group tends not to utilize services available. Thus, while the elderly comprise approximately 10% of the U.S. population, they account for only 2% of the client load in outpatient groups (Kucharski, White, & Schratz, 1979). Part of the reason may be found in this group's documented reluctance to utilize new services (Barney & Neukom, 1979). Hence, it may be more likely that a greater proportion of uncooperative or reluctant patients is obtained from the elderly cohort relative to younger age groups.

It has been suggested that instead of cultivating a special field in this area, specific characteristics of a given individual

The authors are with the Lincoln Family Practice Program, Lincoln, Nebraska.

161

should be examined (Kastenbaum, 1978). For example, rather than studying depression and its treatment in the elderly population, the focus should be on a case study of the depressed individual and the specific therapeutic regimen selected for him or her. Whereas case studies may be limited in their contribution to the development of scientific theory, they do provide useful information. Case studies fulfill a valuable need of explicating the effective procedural components in therapy (e.g., isolating the influence of physical concomitants, medication, and social support factors in the treatment of the individual patient).

The following case study is presented to clarify some of the issues associated with managing the uncooperative elderly patient. This case study is unique in that it documents the contribution of a physician-psychologist team in the case management. Working as a team facilitated the care of the total patient and avoided difficulties inherent in either professional attempting to individually handle the patient. The case study is presented in two parts in which the details of the case analysis and management are followed by the exploration of more general concepts that are illustrated by this case.

CASE ANALYSIS AND MANAGEMENT

This 60-year-old married female has been followed for six months. She initially presented with multiple somatic complaints and clear evidence of depression which was strongly denied by the patient. During the first three months of frequent office visits and laboratory tests, her symptoms were assessed to rule out any organic etiology and to determine appropriate medical management strategies. During the next three months, the systematic medical management of the patient was combined with regular psychotherapy sessions. The following summary characterizes the management issues presented by this case.

Assessment Phase

This patient first presented with increased bowel gas with heartburn. She related that she had been treated by another physician for hypertension but did not wish to disclose the physician's name, nor did she want him to know that she was being seen by another physician. The patient had previous prescriptions for Dalmane and Valium for sleep problems and nervousness.

Additional difficulty in assessing this patient was created by her multiple somatic complaints, including problems with her upper dentures, sinus drainage, drooping upper left eyelid, intermittent dizziness, occassional chest pain, constipation, mass in her right labia minora, minor body aches, weakness, and recent weight loss. The patient also indicated decreased appetite, decreased libido, sleep difficulties, sadness, worries about family problems, and some suicidal thoughts (no suicidal plans). She did not feel understood by her children or her spouse, and her husband's alcoholism seemed to play a large part of many family stresses. A phone call from one of the patient's daughters revealed the family's concern over the patient's multiple complaints and episodes of false crises. The daughter also revealed that the patient utilized multiple over-the-counter medications.

Past history included a left mastectomy for breast cancer seven years earlier and a cholecystectomy four years prior to the patient's initial visit. Family history was positive for heart problems, hypertension, stroke, diabetes, and emotional problems.

Initial medical exam resulted in a diagnosis of viral pharyngitis, reflux esophagitis, hypertension (poorly controlled), intermittent dizziness of unknown etiology, low-grade tachycardia, and depression.

Subsequent vists were utilized to sort out these problems and to rule out organic etiology. Assessment was complicated by additional body complaints at each visit and by the patient's absolute denial of a possibility of depression.

Lab tests demonstrated normal thyroid function, monilial vaginitis, slightly depressed electrolytes, Class I Pap test, and normal hematology. EKG displayed normal sinus rhythm with nonspecific ST-T changes. Chest X-ray was within normal limits except for some spinal osteoarthritis.

Over the first three months, the patient's blood pressure remained poorly controlled, tachycardia persisted, and weight loss continued. Oral potassium supplement corrected the hypokalemia. The monilial vaginitis was treated and Premarin cream was provided for vulva dryness. Her labial mass was excised revealing a calcified blood clot. Antacid therapy corrected the patient's esophagitis. Dizziness was thought to be secondary to orthostatic changes from the blood pressure medicine. However, a 24-hour Holter monitor was performed revealing intermittent sinus tachycardia with significant ST segment depression, not correlated with diagnostic symptoms.

Treatment Phase

At this time, a decision was made to discontinue the patient's hydralazine and to initiate beta-blocker therapy. An attempt was made to discontinue the patient's use of Dalmane and Valium and to discourage her use of over-the-counter medications. Since her depressive symptoms had persisted and the patient was concerned that she may have cancer, a low-dose antidepressant medication was initiated at bedtime. A decision was also made to refer the patient to the psychologist in the clinic for psychotherapy.

Psychotherapy focused on the development of self-management strategies including assertiveness with her spouse and other family members and cognitive strategies such as reframing and use of positive-coping statements. The patient resisted attempts to explore past experiences and coping patterns, claiming that such efforts made her feel fatigued and drowsy. Thus, psychotherapy was much more supportive than confrontive.

Results

The patient's medical record was reviewed and monthly frequencies of office visits, calls, and laboratory tests were obtained. Data for the three months of the Assessment and Treatment Phases were averaged, producing a rate per month score. These data are shown in Table 1, along with t-values obtained by performing a t-test for dependent measures on the paired monthly Assessment and Treatment scores. The only statistically significant difference obtained was in the reduction of office calls. Reduction in mean number of office visits and laboratory tests were in the expected direction, but

Table 1   Monthly rate of office visits, office calls, and laboratory tests during three month Assessment and Treatment Phases.[a]

	Office Visits	Office Calls	Laboratory Tests
Assessment Phase	2.0	3.0	5.3
Treatment Phase	1.0	.33	1.3
t Value	1.73	3.02*	1.92

[a]The df's for all tests were 2

*$p < 0.05$

failed to reach statistically significant levels. Perhaps more importantly, these reductions were accompanied by substantial clinical improvement that was not quantified.

The patient's clinical improvement during the treatment phase included the following: Having initally come to the clinic in a wheelchair, on recent visits she was walked unaided or with the use of a cane. Her mood was considerably improved and she was able to generate more positive coping statements. Crying, which had been present during the assessment phase, was absent, and she showed substantial insight into the dynamics of the relationship with her alcoholic husband and her family members. The number of somatic complaints decreased, she was able to gain weight, and blood pressure became well controlled.

GENERAL CONCEPTS

Several important concepts are illustrated by this case study. Gentry (1978) indicates that factors such as the physician-patient relationship are important determinants of the extent of somatopsychic reactions, with poor relationships exacerbating psychological problems resulting from illness. In this case, it was clear that the patient was "doctor shopping" to a degree and presented with multiple somatic complaints. It is possible that the earlier physician-patient relationship was of poor quality and that perhaps the patient had been stereotyped as a "crock" and adequate medical assessment and treatment had not been provided, thus exacerbating the symptoms initially presented. When the stereotypical attitude was overcome, the physician was able to identify legitimate medical and psychological issues, systematic care was provided, and both the true medical conditions and the patient's underlying depression were more readily apparent and treatable.

The patient was uncooperative several times early in treatment. For example, the patient did not completely fill out the admission history form. Neither would she reveal the name of her previous physician nor did she want him to know she was being seen by another physician. She consistently denied depression and refused antidepressant medications early in treatment and made multiple office calls. A close physician-psychologist relationship was helpful in managing such a patient. Monthly visits were scheduled so that the psychologist was able to schedule a visit following the physician's medical exam. This scheduling gave the psychologist the additional credibility necessary in overcoming this patient's resistance. The physician was able to obtain the patient's compliance with antidepressant medication by suggesting that its intent was to help her sleep. Thus, the patient was able to stop her reliance on Dalmane and Valium and at the same time obtain a more appropriate medication. This is an interesting example of an elderly patient's being more willing to accept a medical explanation and treatment (insomnia-sleeping pill) than a psychological explanation and treatment (depression-antidepressant).

Frequently, the elderly have a bias against admitting the need for counseling and have a greater need to maintain a strong, self-sufficient identity (Haggerty, 1983). This bias was demonstrated in this case study in several ways. The patient strongly denied depression throughout the Assessment Phase and still denies the true impact of the antidepressant medication. The patient resists any attempts in psychotherapy to review past conflicts. In the face of this resistance, psychotherapy has been presented as more of a self-help coping process, a strategy that has helped to circumvent the patient's bias. Thus, although the need for mental health services is especially evident in later life, the availability, or at least the utilization, of such services is less than that for other groups (Butler & Lewis, 1977) and speical efforts are required to obtain the cooperation of uncooperative elderly patients.

This patient is also a good example of how some elderly may use conversation concerning their health status to gain attention from others in the short run but find that they receive less attention and interaction from others in the long run (Plutchik & Conte, 1971). This patient had repeatedly used somatic complaints to gain attention from family and previous physicians, only to have her family tire of the false crises and grow less sympathetic, and to have the physicians overlook some true medical issues and possible treatments. Had this state of affairs continued, the patient's depression would have most likely deepened and her medical problems grown more acute, ultimately requiring hospitalization and more intensive therapeutic efforts. Instead, this patient was provided a good, stable relationship with an element of social support and encouragement that contributed to her successful coping and adaptation (Gentry, 1978). One must be aware that the physical complaints of the elderly may alienate others and diminish the social support network so important for the maintenance of good health (Wisocki, Handen, & Wisocki, 1982).

As the same time the patient was being offered such a supportive relationship, the physician and psychologist were able to support each other and pursue the best care for the patient. The physician working alone may have succumbed to time pressures or the previous stereotype and not pursued a more systematic medical evaluation and psychological approach. The psychologist working alone may not have been able to overcome the resistance and/or may have missed the significant medical issues, perhaps passing a potential cardiac problem as a mere consequence of the psychological condition. With this patient, once the medical issues were addressed, the patient's depression could be identified and managed along with some of the family dynamics.

Interestingly enough, once the medical problems were clarified and treated, the patient's depression emerged as the principal problem, and that was treated. But as the depression resolved, a third level emerged. The persistent problems associated with family dynamics emerged as an important issue. Given the patient's infrequent office visits and the inaccessibility of the family to therapy, this patient's medical and psychological condition was probably resolved to the extent possible. Unfortunately, the patient may remain vulnerable to future problems until the family issues can be addressed. In part, this patient's problems are the result of environmental disruptions in her living situation that have not been buffered by adequate resources, such as support groups. This follows from a stress adaptation model (Palmore, Cleveland, Wowlin, Ramm, & Siegler, 1979), which also suggests that development of such supports may minimize the negative impact of future disruptions. These levels (medical, psychological, social) of the current problem are a good illustration of Engel's (1980) concept of the biopsychosocial model, a model which provides additional insight into the problems of the elderly.

CONCLUSION

Though the uncooperative elderly patient poses many unique problems to the health care professions, this case study supports the effectiveness of the physician-psychologist team in addressing some of these issues. The physician member was able to systematically identify the true medical conditions among the multiple complaints presented and direct appropriate medical treatment. Once these conditions were addressed, the patient's underlying depression was even more evident and was treated with antidepressants and psychotherapy by the psychologist. Throughout the course of treatment, the close communication between physician and psychologist was an important factor in bringing about change in the patient. This communication served as the basis for mutual support necessary in managing a difficult patient, provided a broader data base, and permitted problem solving which assisted working through the case.

Several general issues were illustrated in this case study. The importance of a sound physician-patient relationship was illustrated in that a sound relationship apparently pre-empted additional "doctor shopping" by this patient and facilitated the identification of important medical issues that had previously gone unnoticed. Though this patient denied the role of psychological factors in her illness, she was nontheless convinced to pursue psychotherapy by getting her to focus on the self-help dimension of the work and the importance of maintaining independence. Clearly, this patient used complaints about health in attempts to gain the support of family and the physician. Though this had alienated the family and may have contributed to her previous physician overlooking true medical issues, this patient was managed in such a way that she was given consistent support so that medical and psychological issues could be confronted.

Finally, several levels of the problem were explored, including medical, psychological, and social, and each was found to be important. In the current case, though medical and psychological issues were successfully identified and treated, residual problems in family dynamics and the lack of a good support system may make this patient more vulnerable to future problems. However, in having gone through a biopsychosocial model, considerable information has been gathered, utilized, and evaluated so that future efforts to help maintain the health of this individual patient are more likely to meet with success.

REFERENCES

Barney, J.L., & Neukom, I.E. (1979). Use of arthritis care by the elderly. *Gerontologist, 19,* 548–554.

Butler, R., & Lewis, M. (1977). *Aging and mental health.* St. Louis, MO: Mosby.

Engel, G.L. (1980). The clinical application of the biopsychosocial model. *The American Journal of Psychology, 137,* 535–544.

Gentry, W.D. (1978). Psychosomatic issues in assessment. In M. Storandt, I.C. Siegler, & M.F. Elias (Eds.), *The clinical psychology of aging* (pp. 181–194). New York: Plenum Press.

Haggerty, A.D. (1983). A non-traditional psychotherapy model for the elderly. *Clinical Gerontologist, 2* (2), 53–55.

Kastenbaum, R. (1978). Personality theory, therapeutic approaches, and the elderly client. In M. Storandt, I.C. Siegler, & M.F. Elias (Eds.), *The clinical psychology of aging* (pp. 199–224). New York: Plenum Press.

Kuscharski, L.T., White, R.M., Jr., & Schratz, M. (1979). Age bias referral for psychological assistance, and the private physician. *Journal of Gerontology, 34,* 423–428.

Palmore, E., Cleveland, W., Nowlin, J., Ramm, D., & Siegler, I. (1979). Stress and adaptation in later life. *Journal of Gerontology, 34,* 24–32.

Plutchik, R., Weiner, M., & Conte, H. (1971). Studies of body images: I. Body worries and body discomforts. *Journal of Gerontology, 26,* 334–350.
Wisocki, P.A., Handen, B., & Wisocki, S.J. (1982). *The relationship of social support to the health of community-dwelling elderly.* Paper presented at the meeting of the Association for Advancement of Behavior Therapy, Los Angeles, CA.
Wisocki, P.A., & Mosher, P. (1982). The elderly: An understudied population in behavioral research. *International Journal of Behavioral Geriatrics, I,* 5–14.

Chapter 19:
Advice for the Internist

Walsh gives many practical suggestions on how to get the patient to come in for treatment and medication compliance. The suggestions for interviewing and managing paranoids are particularly useful. However, his recommendation of anti-coagulant therapy is highly controversial, and has been the topic of a previous *CG* special issue:

I (3) 3–13

Tips for the physician's office practice with the aged have also been covered:

II (1) 56–58

The Uncooperative Geriatric Patient

Arthur C. Walsh, MD

Frequently many difficult situations arise in the treatment of geriatric patients. Following are some examples with methods of coping with them that we have found useful.

1. *It is difficult for the relatives to even get the patient to consent to see a physician, especially a psychiatrist.* I have found it effective to advise the relative to focus on the patients physical symptoms—a pain in the leg, abdomen or elsewhere and say "this doctor may be able to relieve that problem for you." This is not really a falsehood for often such symptoms result from emotional strain and are relieved by appropriate treatment. On his first visit one man hovered hostilely in the waiting room for some time before grudgingly coming into the consulting room. We barely got him into therapy but a year later he returned in a very friendly manner making our efforts seem well worthwhile as the family had been at their wits' ends as to how to care for him. The pains these people have disappear completely as a rule. This finding was so impressive and occured so often that I wrote a short paper on the phenomenon.

2. *The patient refuses to take the pills.* You may instruct the relatives to use the liquid form and put it in juice, milk or pudding. We try to avoid this but in a difficult situation it is the most ethical approach since to deny a paranoid older patient such relief would result in the very thing he would not want— institutionalization in a nursing home or State Hospital.

3. *Hesitant, suspicious or fearful patients.* Gain their confidence in the first interview by not rushing it, by careful and patient listening and by showing plenty of genuine sympathy

Dr. Walsh is Clinical Assistant Professor of Psychiatry, University of Pittsburgh, and Psychiatric Consultant, Veterans Administration Medical Center, Pittsburgh, PA.

and understanding. You can even take the patient's side when feasible in a disagreement with the relatives to show you are on the patient's side and out to help him. Thus you can gradually gain his cooperation and persuade him to take his medicine or be hospitalized or do whatever is necessary for his best care. We have found it very helpful to have a co-therapist, such as a nurse or social worker, who will talk with the patient while the doctor takes the history from the relatives and determines the character and extent of the problem. This therapist not only gathers more data but more importantly gains the confidence and dispels the fears of the patient which makes the later interview with the doctor easier and more relaxed. The atmosphere is more that of a family or social gathering rather than a visit to the doctor and avoids the situation where the patient is sitting in the waiting room silently wondering what the relatives are telling the doctor about him! Also much more information about the patient and family is gathered in this way and this can be very helpful in the overall treatment program. In some situations the order can be reversed with the patient being interviewed first by the doctor and the relatives by the co-therapist. In fact each visit can be handled in this way until the situation is well in hand.

4. *Acutely disturbed or paranoid patients.* In an emergency situation it is often best to give an injection of a neuroleptic such as haloperiodol, in relatively small doses since older people can be quite sensitive to it, at fairly frequent intervals until the patient is calm enough to be controlled by oral medication in liquid or pill form. This problem usually occurs in the emergency room but could happen at home or in a nursing home. Injections can sometimes be avoided by using liquid preparations since they take effect faster than pills.

5. *Long-term problems of paranoia, agitation or combativeness.* Here the neuroleptics are invaluable but must be carefully used in older patients. Haloperidol .25 mg. b.i.d. (sometimes even a smaller dose) is a good beginning dose and can be increased as required. It has less effect on the blood pressure and heart than the less potent phenothiazines but has more tendency to cause extrapyramidal reactions. Medications may be avoided or their dose kept to a minimum by having a calm and understanding caretaker to soothe the patient's fears and offer ressurance.

6. *Conflicts between family and patient and between family members.* Therapy with them all, singly and together, is most helpful and indeed essential in some situations for a successful outcome. Here again the use of a co-therapist can be very helpful. The relatives often overreact to a paranoid parent and can be taught to avoid unnecessary confrontations. Oedipal conflicts and sibling rivalry of long duration can be recognized and gently dealt with easing the tensions for the whole family and this in itself can be very therapeutic for the patient. This in turn helps the relatives and other caretakers, thereby reversing a vicious cycle.

7. *Persisting organic brain syndrome with confusion.* When the above measures fail to give a satisfactory solution and the patient remains confused then a trial of anticoagulant therapy can be offered, provided there are no absolute contraindications. We have found this to be a very effective treatment in many patients, sometimes even with dramatic improvement. If the patient is going to benefit he should show improvement in the first two to three months of a trial of therapy. There is a risk of serious bleeding but I have found patients to be actually safer on anticoagulant therapy than without it because they are continually at risk with their senility progressing and causing them to fall and break a hip or injure themselves in other ways. In contrast, when the treatment is successful they become more stable on their feet, eat better and are generally healthier and happier. I have found that even though the memory does not improve in some patients their dispostion almost always does and this allows them to relax more, less tranquilizers are required and they are much more easily cared for which is a great benefit to the relatives as well as the patient.

REFERENCES

1. Walsh AC: Hypochondriasis associated with organic brain syndrome: a new approach to therapy. J. Am Geriatrics Soc, 24: 430–431, 1976.

2. Walsh AC, Walsh BH, Melaney C: Senile-presenile dementia: follow-up data on an effective psychotherapy-anticoagulant regimen. J Am Geriatrics Soc, 26:467–470, 1978.

3. Aker, JB, Walsh AC and Beam JR: Mental Capacity: Medical and Legal Aspects of Aging. Shepard's/McGraw-Hill. Colorado Springs, Co, 1977.

Chapter 20:
The Case for One-To-One Nursing Assessment

The authors return to the basic premise of this volume: uncooperativeness is a label that staffs place on patients. The label then influences both staff and patient behavior in a vicious circle.

Raber, Lamboo and Mitchell-Pedersen have developed a way to break that cycle: assigning one nurse to be all day with a patient for the assessment. The case of a 57 year old female stroke patient illustrates both the staff's frustration with patient behavior and how the one-on-one assessment effected a therapeutic change of perspective: how the staff saw the patient and how the patient saw the staff.

The final chapter of this volume is upbeat: humanism and efficiency are partners because the best way to save the staff's time is to have the staff spend more time with the patients.

177

From Duckling to Swan

Wendy Chusid Raber, RN, BSN
Faye Lamboo, LPN
Lynne Mitchell-Pederson, RN, MEd

Health care workers of all disciplines readily label patients. This can be convenient shorthand but often labels such as "aggressive," "confused," "disruptive," or "inappropriate" create assumptions about patients and expectations of behaviour. Staff behaviour then reflects the patient's label, reinforcing the "problem" behaviour. Any attempt to analyze the behaviour and detect its cause and meaning are soon lost.

We are attempting to halt this pattern by developing a one to one assessment of the patient for at least a full day period. Trust is created and the nurse can come to appreciate the meaning behind the behaviour for each patient. A case presentation will show how a plan of care can be designed to fit the needs of both staff and patient.

This approach to care has been developed on a 40 bed unit in the Department of Geriatric Medicine at St. Boniface General Hospital, an 850 bed tertiary care facility. The patient population consist of those who are acutely ill, those admitted for rehabilitation, and those awaiting transfer to a personal care home.

CASE STUDY

Mary* is a single, 57 year old woman recently admitted to our hospital for rehabilitation following a stroke. Prior to this admission Mary lived independently with a 22 year old son as

---

The authors are affiliated with St. Boniface Hospital, Winnipeg, Manitoba.

*Not her real name

her dependent, despite the fact that she is an obese, diabetic woman who had a previous stroke 6 years ago.

From the outset Mary was viewed as "problematic" to the staff, constantly "calling out," banging on the walls and side-rails or throwing herself out of her wheelchair onto the floor. At times, Mary refused to eat or drink. Mary's noisy calling and banging at night kept many other patients awake, leaving nurses feeling helpless and frustrated. Staff frustration and anger with Mary were increasing daily. The worse Mary acted, the more impatient staff became.

Initial attempts to solve the problems with Mary were fruitless. Many staff and family conferences were held, including nurses, occupational therapists, a psychologist, physician, and social worker. A medical assessment suggested that her agitation was due to depression. Several antidepressant medications were tried to no avail. It was difficult to determine Mary's level of functioning despite testing by an occupational therapist. Discussions at several multidisciplinary case conferences produced divergent opinion over apparently straightforward issues such as whether she could rise from a chair. Some said she could not, others reported having seen her do this.

In a last ditch attempt to solve the problem, another conference was held with a psychologist, who pointed out the lack of clear information. We decided to have a nurse spend one day with Mary to assess her strengths and limitations. During this day the nurse encouraged Mary to make choices and take control. As the day progressed we watched Mary enjoy a picnic in the park and baking with other patients, where she even suggested variations in the recipe. For the first time Mary slept through the night without "banging" or "calling out." The next day she was alert, oriented, and chatting with others. In turn staff reinforced this behaviour by complimenting Mary and socializing with her. What happened during that day was that staff changed how they saw Mary and Mary's behaviour changed accordingly.

Once Mary saw her nurse as someone who listened and heard how lonely she was, of how difficult it was for her to face recovery from a stroke a second time, then Mary began to trust staff and her behaviour changed. For example, she had initially refused to open her eyes. After the nurse's one-to-one day with her, she was comfortable enough to keep her eyes open. Staff began to value Mary's strengths and appreciate her past accomplishments in life. For instance, they learned about her courage in having raised an illegitimate son alone. They recognized her fortitude when they learned that she had worked for many years under rugged conditions as a cook in a bush camp. But most of all, staff developed pride in having been able to help Mary.

THE ONE-TO-ONE APPROACH

We now realize that the key intervention in Mary's case was the "one nurse to one patient" approach which later proved useful for other patients who were regarded as difficult to manage.

We have identified the sequence of events which led to our "one-to-one" approach. Once a problem is recognized, a Case Conference is held with all disciplines to gather information, including acknowledgement of the patient's recent losses. This enables staff to begin viewing the "uncooperative patient" as an individual.

On determining that a "one-to-one" day might be useful, a staff member is chosen. Although no prescription or recipe can be given there are common elements to look for when identifying the nurse. These include interest, flexibility, creativity, and the ability to be nonjudgemental. It is preferable if the nurse volunteers, indicating her interest in the challenge. If the nurse is reluctant it is unlikely that she will succeed. By flexibility, we mean that the nurse must be able to discard preconceived notions of what should be done or of goals that must be accomplished according to a time schedule.

The nurse may have to be creative in helping the patient plan the day, especially if the patient has been institutionalized for a long time and does not realize that 'outside the hospital' activities are available or that hospital routines are not written in stone. Lastly, the nurse must be nonjudgemental, and be able to respect the patient's values. In addition to these four attributes, the nurse must allow the patient to determine the agenda. That is, she must lose her need to lead. She must be able to follow and support.

After the "one-to-one" day has been carried out, the care plan is revised and evaluated based on the new information obtained during the day including the patient's preferences and newly discovered strengths and interests.

Why Does It Work?

What happens during a one-to-one day? The nurse simply focuses on developing what is commonly called a "therapeutic relationship." Often we assume that such a relationship has been established when this may not be true at all. The care plan, evaluation and follow-up develop from this relationship of trust. Mary's change of behaviour after this "one-to-one" day was not anticipated. Behavioural change was not our goal initially—observation was! By the end of a one-to-one day observation period, we recognized that Mary's behaviour was part of her depression and identified Mary's many capabilities.

We want to be clear that observation does not mean a more finely tuned assessment form. Focusing on questions rather than following the patient's lead would defeat the purpose. Yet, at the end of the day with Mary, a number of assessment questions could have been answered with the wealth of information gleaned. What seems to be a key element in the relationship is the patient's developing awareness of being valued and understood. What our approach really boils down to is that the nurse treats the patient as a valued and respected adult human being.

Did It Work With Others?

Over the last 22 months this one-to-one approach has been tried on five patients. The time nurses spent with a patient ranged from 1 to 3 days. (see Figure I).

In our 5 cases the changes are lasting. We maintained contact with our first patient (A) for 22 months, through our Day Hospital. Patient B was followed for 21 months after this approach was used and the positive effects were still evident. Patients C & D have since died, but not before the positive changes were seen to last 2 and 3 months respectively. Patient E spent 3 days with a "one-to-one" nurse and the positive effects were enjoyed for 4 months until her discharge.

FIGURE I

Patient	Sex	Diagnosis	Behaviour Before "One-to-One" day
A (Mary)	F	Stroke	- banging on walls and side-rails - refusing to stand or open eyes
B	M	Diabetis (R) B/K amputation	- Sexual remarks and advances - throwing tray and dishes on floor
C	F	Myxedema	- aggression - verbal and physical - swinging cane - spitting, swearing - refusing to wash
D	M	Ca prostate dementia	- swearing - yelling - hitting out - refusing A.M. care
E	F	PVD Leg ulcers agitated depression	- yelling - refusing to wash - paranoid delusions

FIGURE 1 (continued)

Length of "One-to-One" time	Patient Behaviour after "One-to-One" day	Staff Behaviour after "One-to-One" day	Length of Follow-up
1 day	- socializing, participating in unit activities - walking independently with open eyes	- asking to be assigned to patient - visiting with patient in spare time	22 months (through Day Hospital)
1 day	- Fewer comments and advances - Began to display sense of humour	- Less reaction to sexual overtures	21 months (through Day Hospital)
2 days	- aggressive behaviour ceased - chatting, laughing and joking with staff	- asking to be assigned to her (became a "favourite patient") - mourned her death	2 months (died)
1 day	- aggressive behaviour ↓	- changed routine of care to "suit" patient... ↓ need for him to resist care	3 months (died)
3 days	- seemed calmer - chatting freely and came to trust staff	- willingly spent time with her - changed routine and ↓ need to resist care	4 months (discharged)

Bearing in mind that no causal relationship has been established, and the limited insight provided by only 5 cases, this approach appears to have influenced patients' behaviour, staff behaviour and staff perception of the patient. We have tentatively categorized these outcomes of our cases into 3 areas (see Figure II):

    I. *Changes in patient behaviour* included an increase in participation in their care and decreased so-called "attention-seeking" behaviours, such as calling out.

   II. *Staff behaviour changes* were typified by an increase in the time staff chose to spend with the patients and more importantly a desire to be assigned to patients previously seen as "undesirable."

  III. *Changes in the staff perceptions of the patients* were evident in that staff began to recognize the value of uniqueness in behaviour that was previously seen as negative. For example, Mary's refusal to stand on her feet was later understood as her attempt to control some area of her life.

ADMINISTRATIVE ISSUES

How did we justify the cost of this approach? An additional nurse had to be scheduled to work this day, so there is a monetary factory. What justifies it most in our eyes is the apparent increase in staff satisfaction with their jobs. In short, all nurses want to do a good job and see that their patients are contented. Frequently patients whose behaviour is perceived to be demanding create frustration and exhaustion for the staff involved. Eventually, working under those circumstances leads to low staff morale (see Figure III). According to Reinhardt (1973), low staff morale has been linked to absenteeism and staff turnover. Nurses who quit may be more costly than we realize. In our department, hiring one nurse costs over $1600.00 for orientation alone. Not all nurses however, will quit because of frustration, but those who do *not* may present the picture we have all met of the embittered, desensitized nurse who provides anything but quality care.

Decreased staff satisfaction costs; both in money and in quality. Figure IV lays out the process whereby as staff frustration decreases, their satisfaction increases. They are happier, resulting in less turnover and sick time and thereby less dollars. The result is more consistent caregivers, happier patients and the cycle continues.

FIGURE II

1. Changes in patient behaviour.
2. Changes in staff behaviour.
3. Changes in staff perception of patients.

FIGURE III

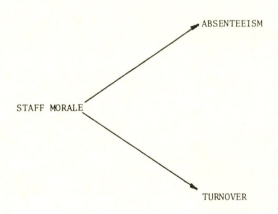

STAFF MORALE

ABSENTEEISM

TURNOVER

Reinhardt, R.L. (1983), "Employee Moral - A Job Factor", Nursing Homes.

FIGURE IV

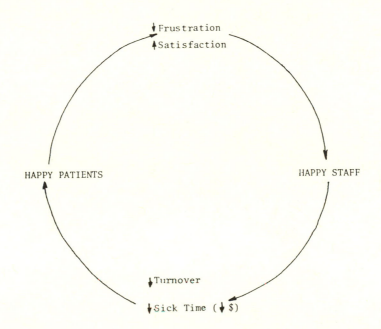

Nurses who have participated in this approach, have found it to be an educational experience that carries over to the care of *all* their patients and frequently infects the rest of the staff.

DO WE LABEL PATIENTS?

The story of this "problem" patient may have a familiar ring to many. The title of this article is an analogy for the change in our perception of our so-called "problem" patients. Sometimes we label people "disruptive," "inappropriate," "manipulative," or "uncooperative." These labels create assumptions about patients and how they will behave. Because staff expect "problem" behaviour, that very result occurs. We came to the realization that we were unwittingly viewing these patients as "ugly ducklings." After our approach changed, so did our perception and we began to see them instead as "beautiful swans."

REFERENCES

Reinhardt, R.L. 1983. Employee Morale—A Job Factor. *Nursing Homes.*

Index

ABANDONMENT, feeling of, 64
ABC CHART, 123–124,126
ABREACTION, see ventilation
ABUSE (elder patients abusing staff),
    43–57,133,145–154
ADMINISTRATIVE issue, 185–187
AFFECTIVE DISORDERS, see de-
    pression, mania
ADL, 49–51
ADVICE, 10
AGGRESSION, see also passive ag-
    gression, 46,136,143,179
AGITATION, 11–12,16,17,25,35–
    40,62–64,75,123,128,143,149,
    174,180
AGNOSIA, 37
AGREEMENT, 10
AIDES, see staff
ALCOHOL, ALCOHOLIC,
    13–15,135
ALERTNESS, see confusion
ALZHEIMER'S DISEASE, see con-
    fusion
AMBULATION, see mobility
ANALYTIC NEUTRALITY, 59
ANGER, 8,11,13–22,43,56,93,104,
    115,133,141
ANIMAL, see pet
ANTECEDENT-BEHAVIOR-
    CONSEQUENCE chart,
    123–124, 126
ANTI-COAGULANT, 171,175
ANXIETY, see agitation
APATHY, 21,123,143
APPEARANCE of patient, 66
APRAXIA, 37, 122
ARGUING with patient, 10
ART THERAPY, 129
ASSESSMENT, 23–40,69,81–82,

122–123,127–128,158,162–164,
    177–188
AUDIO TAPES, 77
AUTHORITARIAN psychiatrists, 14
AUTONOMY of patient, 6–9
    see also dependency, helplessness

BALANCE accounts, 90–91,94–96
BATH, 116
BEHAVIOR THERAPY, 119–128,
    149,159,164
    see also Cognitive-Behavior Therapy
BENDER-GESTALT TEST, 26
BEREAVEMENT, 63,92–93,140,142
BIPOLAR DISORDER
    see mania
BITING, 43
BLACK patient, 75–78
BLADDER infection, 112
BLAME, 3–16
    see also label
BLINDNESS, see vision
BLOOD PRESSURE, see cardio-
    vascular
BODY COMPLAINTS, see somatic
    complaints
BRAIN DAMAGE, see confusion
BRAIN SCANNING, see CT
BREAKFAST meetings with patient,
    79–83
BURNOUT, 131

CANTANKEROUSNESS, see anger,
    agitation
CARDIO-VASCULAR DISEASE,
    19–22,39,81,163–164
CAREGIVERS, see also family, staff,
    75–77,113–119
CAT SCANNING 35,39,122